THE
INTELLECTUAL
BACKGROUND OF THE
REVOLUTION IN
SOUTH AMERICA
1810-1824

Gutzon Borglum
STATUETTE OF SIMON BOLIVAR
New York. The Hispanic Society of America

THE
INTELLECTUAL
BACKGROUND OF THE
REVOLUTION IN
SOUTH AMERICA
1810-1824

BY

BERNARD MOSES, Ph.D., LL.D.

RUSSELL & RUSSELL

1966

PREFACE

This sketch might have become a book if the light had not failed. In its present form, it may suggest to some one the task of making a more extensive presentation of the subject. Hitherto the events of the discovery, of the conquest, and of the war of emancipation have especially engaged the attention of writers on Spanish South America. The two hundred and fifty years of dull colonial existence lacked the movement requisite for an attractive story. A continuous chronological history of the period is doomed to be wanting in dramatic quality, for life in the colonies as a whole was not dramatic; but the long waste stretches were broken here and there by stirring episodes, such as the mining life of Potosí, the rebellion of Tupac Amaru, the expulsion of the Jesuits, the uprising of the *comuneros* in New Granada, and the conflict with the Portuguese in Brazil. By reason of this character of colonial life, the history, in order to be interesting, or conformable to reality, or anything more than a spiritless chronicle, must present the events grouped about certain conspicuous centres of action. It is not a consecutive story like the history of France or the history of any civilized country with a centralized government.

The history of the dependencies during the struggle for political emancipation shows a degree of unity superior to that of the previous period. The patriots in all parts of the colonial territory were in pursuit of a common end, and in this undertaking they were in conflict with the royalists. This conflict is the prominent and characteristic fact of the fourteen years of the revolution, but the patriots' first successes were followed by the temporary triumph of the royalists. Nevertheless the military events of the period may be

set forth in systematic order. Beginning in the extremes of the colonial
territory, Venezuela and Argentina, the
victorious patriots advanced in the north
from Venezuela into New Granada; in
the south, from Argentina into Chile;
then, from these two points the two
forces, under Bolívar and San Martín,
moved upon Perú, the territory of the
most ancient viceroyalty of South
America and the last stronghold of
Spanish power. Here the patriots' victory was complete, the Spanish forces
were scattered, and the ancient dependencies were delivered over to men who
had then most of the practical lessons
in governing still to learn.

Behind the practical enterprises of
the revolution there was a body of
thought and opinion, forming the intellectual background of the revolution.
It is the purpose of the following brief
chapters to sketch this background;
another hand may fill it in with the
proper colours.

CONTENTS

I

The Spanish-American revolution, like other revolutions, offers two general subjects for contemplation. One comprehends the external acts, the formation of armies, the military campaigns and the overthrow of the old political organization. The other comprehends the mental attitude of the revolutionists, the expression of revolt in the literature of the period, and the application of new political doctrines in legislation. The first of these subjects in connection with the South American revolution has engaged the attention of many writers, who have described the early movements of the revolutionists, the campaigns of Bolívar, the passage of the Andes by San Martín, and the final triumph of the patriots in Perú.

The following pages do not deal especially with the external events of the revolution, but present the colonial mind in the process of acquiring ideas of liberty: in a word, the intellectual background of the struggle for emancipation.

The difference between the colonial mind and the mind of the ancestral nation is largely the result of the colonists' environment, of their great expectations, and of their freedom from the social conventions of their mother country. Under these influences the colonial mind acquires its peculiar character. In the presence of nature at the frontier of civilization, where no artificial institutions or ancient social forms contribute to maintain personal or class distinctions, where property is generally the result of the personal efforts of the owners, where the amounts held by the several inhabitants do not vary greatly, there exists a natural tendency towards the development of

the democratic spirit. The struggle
with nature, moreover, stimulates the
growth of practical sense, of individual
independence, and of the idea of
equality.

An illustration of this influence of
frontier life is found in the early British colonies in America, where few or
no counteracting regulations had been
imposed by the home government. In
the Spanish dependencies, on the other
hand, the normal influence of the frontier was checked and modified by restrictions imposed by the government in
Spain. These restrictions tended to nullify the forces making for equality.
Among these restrictions were the laws
creating a titled nobility, the subjection of Indians to feudal dependence
on *encomenderos*, and the vassalage of
encomenderos under the king. Influences proceeding from these sources
stayed the normal intellectual emancipation of the colonists, but in spite of
governmental interference their ideals

and aspirations gradually drifted away from the Spanish standards. This psychological change was, however, much slower in the Spanish colonies than in the British colonies, owing in part to the fact that instruction in the Spanish-American schools was conducted almost exclusively by the clergy, who entertained the same ideas and sentiments as their confrères in Spain, and whose influence tended to perpetuate in the colonies the conservatism of the mother country.

A rigid system of instruction was doubtless necessary in order to develop effective intellectual effort under frontier conditions, but the circumstances of colonial life did not justify a scheme of instruction wholly conservative, tending to deprive all minds subject to it of their native individuality. There is no doubt that instruction by the clergy, and particularly by the Jesuits, gave efficiency in a predetermined direction, but it did not emphasize the idea of progress or provide for society that variety of intellectual equipment required to promote the many interests of a well-balanced and progressive commonwealth. Where the bulk of the vigorous minds in a community are trained exclusively for service in a single sphere there can hardly exist a normal and healthy intellectual life. The predominance of historical, philosophical, and theological investigation and writing, and the comparatively limited amount of thought given to more practical subjects furnish evidence of the one-sidedness and conservatism of mental development in the Spanish colonies.

By the zeal and liberality of the Spanish government in supporting a numerous clergy in America, the colonies were supplied with teachers. The curriculum was usually limited to Latin, mediæval philosophy and theology. Thus clerical instruction in the schools maintained the religious idea in colonial society. The scientific method of thought and the scientific viewpoint, until late in the eighteenth century, were wanting, largely because they were wanting in Spain, and because of the efficiency of ecclesiastical institutions in preventing their development.

The institution most powerful in preventing the use of the scientific method and the acceptance of rational conclusions was doubtless the Inquisition. It was the principal agent of authority for preventing the importation of books, for suppressing free speech, and for prohibiting the spread of heretical doctrines. The almost total absence of communication between the colonies and all European nations, except Spain, permitted the Inquisition and the other religious institutions to have a free hand in shaping the ideas of the colonists. The fact that among the ecclesiastics there was relatively a larger number of educated men than in any other class, contributed to magnify their influence, and to make their views generally dominant.

The ideas of the ecclesiastics, moreover, found expression in the undertaking to civilize the Indians. Concerning this project, the experience of Western nations in dealing with the less developed races has furnished certain definite conclusions. It has shown the futility of opening relations with members of an uncivilized race by a direct attack on their religious ideas and their social traditions. It has made it clear that the most advisable policy with reference to the members of an undeveloped race is not to touch the vital, traditional part of their character or their religion directly but to teach the operations and possible employment of the forces of nature, and the means of making these forces contribute to the satisfaction of society's material needs; while the spiritual transformation is sought through the indirect influence of a changed environment, and by gradually creating new conceptions of life and of the external world.

The persons who formed the governmental policy for civilizing the Indians and those who actually carried on the missionary work attempted a reform at a point where the probability of success was very remote, but the motive of their action was the widely entertained belief that the Indian's submission to baptism effected a radical change in his character. It was this belief that induced the Spanish government to transport large numbers of ecclesiastics to America, and to bear the expense of their maintenance as missionaries to the Indians. The conversion of the Indians was thought to involve not only a change of religion, but also their transformation from barbarism to civilization. The statements by ecclesiastical writers as to the real achievements of this colonial missionary campaign are extravagant exaggerations. " The mature study of the documents shows," to

quote the conclusion of Barros Arana,
" that these statements are nothing more
than inventions destitute of all truth.
The Indians readily allowed themselves
to be baptized either to recover their
liberty or to obtain a gift; but they remained as thoroughly pagan as they
were before; they fled to their districts
at the first opportunity, and returned to
the life of savages without remember-
ing anything of their pretended conversion " (1). Gustave Le Bon affirms
that " when one advances a little into
the study of these conversions, he recognizes that these persons have in fact
only changed the name of their ancient
religion, and not the religion itself;
that in reality the beliefs adopted have
undergone the transformations necessary to put them *en rapport* with the old
beliefs that have been set aside and of
which the new beliefs are only the
simple continuation " (2).

Neither the priests nor the colonists
generally comprehended fully the

strength of tradition in the savage mind; nor had they any adequate appreciation of the time required to evolve civilized men from savages. Concerning this subject, the Jesuits of Paraguay and of the valley of the Orinoco appear to have had a clearer vision than the members of any other class of ecclesiastics. They directed their efforts principally to changing the environment of the Indians, to inducing them to abandon their nomadic state and to accept the conditions of a settled life, to making them accustomed to regular and persistent labour, and thus, by a process that might last many generations, to eliminate their instincts as savages and to develop in them the instincts of civilized persons. But generally throughout the colonies greater stress was laid on teaching Christian doctrine, on repeating the phrases of the catechism, than on creating for the Indians such conditions of living and such other indirect influences as would induce them gradually to adopt the sentiments and ways of enlightened society. The view prevailed that the Indians could be turned from savagism to civilization by precept, and the efforts of centuries and thousands of unselfish lives were wasted in obedience to this false theory.

The general attitude of the colonists towards religion was that of the European Middle Ages. For them there was one true creed, and all persons who accepted it were worthy, and all who failed to do so were unworthy, and ought not to be tolerated in any of the colonial communities. The conduct of the Inquisition in suppressing all other creeds, by any means however cruel, was regarded with a certain popular favour. The auto-da-fé was accepted by the body of the people not merely because it was a diversion in their otherwise uneventful lives, but also because they believed that the church was right in its intolerant suppression of all religious views at variance with its creed, and because of the fear which the Inquisition inspired in them. When the church affirmed that an earthquake was an instance of divine punishment for the sins of the people, that statement settled the question of its origin as far as the popular mind was concerned. This interpretation, the bulk of the people had no disposition to dispute, nor was there any inducement to undertake a scientific examination of the facts. Thus the dictum of the church on facts of nature was popularly accepted as a tenet of religious belief, and, reposing in this faith, each generation passed on to its successor an abiding confidence in ecclesiastical authority.

Supported in their intolerant attitude by the faith of the people, some of the ecclesiastical institutions were disposed to exceed the proper limits of their jurisdiction and to become arrogant in their relation to the inhabitants among whom they were established, and hostile towards the government. Thus the Inquisition sometimes rejected the request of the government for a conciliatory decision where the interests of the two organizations clashed. By its terrorism the Inquisition subdued the spirit of the common man, depriving him of independence not only in thought and utterance, but also in action.

When ecclesiastics, as colonial teachers, turned to instruct the Indians, their curriculum emphasized only the subject of religion. This was inevitable, since it did not appear probable that instruction in Latin would produce advantageous results, yet without a knowledge of this language the other subjects of the clerical curriculum were not available; and there was no ground for supposing that the Indians, with no inheritance in the Christian tradition, could be led far into the mysteries of mediæval philosophy. The missionary was confined to the task of teaching his pupils a new religion; in this way he was led to strike directly at the most vital and permanent element of the Indian's character and traditions, in fact at the root of his individuality and independence.

While it is possible, as in the case of the ecclesiastics, to make more or less clear the mental attitude of any given class in the colonies, it is much more difficult to discover a body of ideas and sentiments, which was the common possession of the whole population. Each of the sharply defined classes of the inhabitants had its peculiar views and aspirations; but a common public opinion, like that which prevailed in the British colonies of North America, did not exist. For example the *encomenderos*, to whom lands had been granted and Indians assigned, by the king, held views that were determined by their position and their interests. They demanded that the Indians should remain in perpetual subordination to them, and that the feudal spirit and the feudal organization of society should be continued indefinitely.

On many points the views of the *encomenderos* were distinctly opposed to the views of the clergy. The clergy represented the missionary elements in Spain's royal policy respecting America, which aimed at the Christianization of the Indians, and their elevation to membership in civilized communities. This policy necessarily involved the ultimate release of the Indians from subordination to the *encomenderos*. The ideal of the clergy, an ideal, however, not strictly followed, contemplated the ultimate freedom of all classes. The purpose of the *encomenderos*, on the other hand, was to retain their place as a dominating class and to develop a limited body of wealthy landholders, whose material prosperity should rest on the servile labour of the Indians.

On the policy of the freedom or slavery of the Indians, there existed a variety of fluctuating opinions. When the early colonists found themselves holding Indians under grants by the king, it satisfied their conscience to assert that the Indians as compared with the Spaniards were another, and a lower, order of beings. The view of the *conquistadores* was that "the Indians were not men, like other men, but simply animals superior to the monkey; that they were slaves by nature " (3). In support of this view they were able to cite the distinguished authority of Aristotle; and Solórzano, the author of *Política indiana* (4) gave it his endorsement. The doctrine thus ceased to be a mere vulgar opinion, and acquired in some sense scientific standing. It was defended in speech and writing, and became so widely accepted that Pope Paul the Third, June 10th, 1537, denounced it as malicious and proceeding from diabolical covetousness. It was, moreover, in sharp contrast with the ideas expressed by the kings of Spain on many occasions, namely, that the American aborigines were equal to the Spanish vassals, and quite as free, and consequently should be masters of their persons and their property (5). There thus arose a conflict of views. The royal view was upheld in America by the greater part of the ecclesiastics and by the lawyers, but the *conquistadores* supported the opposing view. This divergence of opinions was far-reaching in its practical effects, making a contrast between the policy conceived and formulated in Spain and the policy carried out in America.

In the course of time the supreme government departed from its benevolent idealism, and, under the pressure of what appeared to be a practical necessity, in 1609 declared that Indians in rebellion might be made slaves. This order was confirmed by Philip the Fourth, in 1625, and the slaves held under the authority of these decrees were branded with a hot iron, in order that they might be identified in case they

should run away. The fact that some-
what later (1635) the king left the
question of Indian slavery to the dis-
cretion of the viceroy of Perú, indicates
that the secular opinion in America concerning this subject had prevailed; it
became, in fact, gradually more rigid
in theory and merciless in practice. The
abuses under this privilege became so
great that the king was ultimately con-
strained to issue a decree abolishing the
practice of enslaving the Indians. At
length, at the end of the seventeenth
century, as another phase of a vacillat-
ing policy, the supreme government
returned to its original view, as wit-
nessed by a decree issued by Charles
the Second, in 1697, solemnly declaim-
ing that his vassals in the New World
and the Old were equal and ought to
be treated in the same manner.

The owners of mines and *obrajes*, or
manufacturing establishments, were not
less disposed than the *encomenderos* to
hold the Indians in a state of servile

dependence. Their plans involved no idea of improving the status of the subject race; they aimed simply to acquire the greatest possible gain from the Indians' toil; they gave no attention to the disastrous consequences of severe enforced labour on persons unaccustomed to an amount of persistent effort which only civilized men can perform with impunity. The views of the manufacturers coincided essentially with the views of the *encomenderos*, and both were opposed to any change in the status of the Indians that would diminish the prospects of economic advantage.

The soldiers constituted a third class of marked individuality. Their ideas had a comparatively narrow range; they conceived their mission to be to subjugate a people assumed to be hostile, and to cause the power and majesty of the Spanish crown to be respected. Coming from Spain and returning to that country after a service of four or five

years in America, they became interested only to a very limited extent in
the aims and purposes of the permanent
part of the population. They were
often transferred from one province to
another, and were thus prevented from
establishing close relations with the
other classes.

Within this class appeared some of
the noteworthy colonial writers. Ercilla
y Zúñiga is especially prominent among
those of the sixteenth century. His
Araucana, although written only in part
in America, exhibits the reaction of the
author's mind in the presence of the
unfamiliar scenery of Chile and
the frontier warfare with the Arauca-
nian Indians. Primarily designed to
celebrate the achievements of Spanish
arms in America, one of the poem's
striking features is its presentation of a
small and rude people heroically de-
fending its traditional liberty against attacks by Spanish forces. It was exten-
sively read, particularly in Chile, and its

masterful sketches of Colocolo, Caupolicán, Lautaro, Tucapel, and other native chiefs, awakened admiration and sympathy, and magnified the virtue manifest in a struggle for liberty against an oppressive, alien, and hostile power. The lasting influence of this poem on the mind of the colonists may be inferred from the fact that long after the events narrated the colonists were accustomed to give the names of these champions of liberty to their children, and the name of Lautaro was applied to an association formed to advocate colonial emancipation from Spain. To Cieza de León, Bascuñán, Vásquez, Carvallo, and other soldiers the historical literature of Spanish South America is indebted for many of its most important works.

The writings of soldiers on the history of the colonies reveal a rational spirit quite in contrast with the mystical conceptions of ecclesiastics who have written on the same subjects. They recognize that they have to do with events originating in this world, while the priests and the friars in their narratives are disposed to seek the causes of many events in the proceedings of another world or in an arbitrary and incomprehensible divine intervention.

Questions concerning government and other social affairs engaged the colonists' thought, but perhaps less generally than religious topics. There was, moreover, a greater variety of opinions on politics than on religion, but this diversity was only gradually developed. The ideas of liberty and equality presented a sharp contrast to the conservatism supporting class distinctions. The development of this opposition is a conspicuous feature of colonial thought on politics during the period of Spanish domination. The bulk of the creoles and mestizos entertained liberal views, while the Spaniards supported the ideas and policy of the government in Spain. Although it was

generally recognized that the supreme
government neglected to protect colonial interests, the officials, the members
of the clergy, and the holders of commercial or industrial privileges remained loyal to the Spanish administration, and regarded themselves as a
colonial aristocracy. Certain wealthy
creoles, moreover, anxious to acquire
social distinction, identified themselves
with this class; but some of them,
while they supported Spanish rule, were
opposed to that feature of it which
favoured exploiting the colonies for the
benefit of the mother country.

Although the creoles and the mestizos
appeared in revolt against the Spanish
policy and were inclined, under the
normal influences of their position, to
favour freedom and equality, it was
not until late in the period of dependence on Spain that their attitude became
conspicuous. During the greater part
of that period, no considerable number
of the colonists had any adequate con-

ception of political liberty; and their individual liberty was in a very large measure suppressed. The agencies that coöperated to produce this result were the elaborate restrictions imposed by the supreme government, the school instruction conceived and carried out by the clergy, and the vigilant and persecuting Inquisition. Dominated and moulded by forces proceeding from these sources, the colonists made comparatively little real progress; years and decades came and went but scarcely brought them higher aspirations or a broader intellectual vision. Their physical existence acquired certain ameliorations in the course of time but the literary achievements of the eighteenth century show no considerable, if any, advance over the writings of the sixteenth century. And more than this, the high spirit of adventure and the heroic daring which marked their early undertakings by sea and land disappeared after the government had brought into full exercise its restraining and protecting power.

Vigorous and effective popular political thought appears only with the opportunity for popular political action. The British colonists in America turned to public or social affairs sooner than the Spanish colonists, and a principal cause of this, aside from their national character, was the necessity under which they existed of largely governing themselves. The Spanish colonists were under no such necessity, and had no such opportunity, and therefore, with respect to this phase of their life, they remained politically immature; and even for a considerable period after they had achieved independence, their political thought was either vague or visionary, and their practical steps were halting and uncertain.

It must not be supposed, however, that there was no political thought in the Spanish colonies. Such a conclusion would be clearly controverted by the facts. The writings of Matienzo, Solórzano, Escalona, Calvo de la Torre, and León Pinelo present abundant evidence of important thinking on political subjects; but these were men who drew their inspiration largely from their practical administrative activity. They were men of unusual careers; their lives were in striking contrast with the lives of the colonists in general, whose exclusion from governmental offices and all participation in governmental affairs deprived them of incentives to political reflection.

In estimating the quality and characteristics of the colonial mind, one must give weight to the influence of migration. This influence was twofold: in the first place, by a process of selection, it brought together in the New World persons whose average energy was superior to that of their countrymen who continued to reside in the communities which the emigrants had left; in the second place, the persons who immigrated were subject to the stimulus of new scenes and new expectations, which awakened thought and produced a physical activity not experienced by those who had remained on their native soil. Here was the beginning of a difference between the populations of Europe and America. This activity was at first especially directed to matters concerning the immediate interests of the individual persons, while the general social interests were in a large measure neglected. This was partly on account of the isolation in which the colonists lived at first, and partly because these persons, who were by chance brought together into groups, had unlike social traditions that prevented immediate assimilation; and in this state of things there was developed at once a remarkable activity relating to their personal affairs, while the social affairs of the communities remained, at least temporarily, in a condition of stagnation.

II

Influx of
foreign ideas

Throughout the greater part of the colonial period the intellectual individuality of the several social classes in the colonies, as already indicated, persisted and grew more distinctly marked. In the course of time many members of the various classes acquired the idea of political liberty, and these persons were gradually drawn together and formed a political party. This party consisted chiefly of creoles and mestizos, who found themselves opposed by the Spaniards and practically the whole official hierarchy. The liberal views of the creole-mestizo party became more pronounced under the propaganda of liberty proceeding from Europe and the United States.

In the second half of the eighteenth century streams of political ideas poured in upon the hitherto isolated Spanish colonies, especially from two principal sources, France and British North America. The liberal philosophy and revolutionary doctrines of France exerted a powerful influence upon the younger and more cultivated creoles. The young men who went to Europe for the purpose of continuing their studies were stimulated by the free access to books, by the opportunities for research, and by the freedom of speech in the countries visited. They were influenced not merely by the political doctrines that generated the revolution, but also by the spirit of criticism that was directed to the affairs of government and religion. They were drawn by the fashion of the day to study French social philosophy and returned to America full-fledged revolutionists, disciples of the Encyclopedists. In the opinion of José Antonio de Rojas, Abbé Raynal was an *hombre divino,* " the true philosopher, worthy of the praise of the whole world, and particularly of America " (6).

Bernardo O'Higgins was one of these young men. He spent nine years in Europe; the greater part of this period was passed in England, where his political views were developed during his association with Miranda. Teaching algebra and geometry to O'Higgins was for Miranda a means of livelihood, but the emancipation of Spanish America was his absorbing purpose, and it was impossible for him not to be much occupied with his plans, which he naturally communicated to his pupil. He was desirous of attaching so prominent a young person to the cause of independence.

During his residence in Cádiz, where he remained two years, Bernardo was associated with two friars, whose political views had brought them under suspicion. These were José Cortez Madariaga, a Galician, and Juan Pablo Fretes, from Paraguay. O'Higgins arrived in Cádiz from England in 1799, with letters of introduction to these two ecclesiastics, who were agents of Miranda's propaganda. Under the influence of those persons who surrounded him in Cádiz, Bernardo became a member of a group of radicals, including Antonio Nariño, who had formed a compact to work for the liberty of Spanish America. When Viceroy O'Higgins learned that his natural son had espoused the cause of South American independence he suspended the allowance by which Bernardo had met his expenses in England and Spain. At Cádiz Bernardo was entertained by a friend of the Viceroy, Nicolás de la Cruz, who on receiving this information was disposed to put his guest into the street, but finally he agreed to accept, in exchange for continued entertainment, a piano Bernardo had purchased in London and was taking to Chile as a present for his mother. The Viceroy's indignation

over the political attitude assumed by
his son was such that he determined
to disinherit him, but he was prevented
from doing so by his own death in
1801.

Even the government in Spain in the
last years of the eighteenth century had
occasionally liberal views, although not
always disinterested. Its approval of
the liberal commercial code of 1778
was an instance in point. The concession yielded by Spain if not made
on the Spanish government's initiative,
was nevertheless a concession, and inti-
mated to those vitally concerned that
yielding by Spain in certain cases was
not entirely out of the question. The
principal merchants in the colonies were
especially interested in this measure and
in the suggestion that Spain had possibly adopted a new policy that would
favour a more extended local control
over American commercial affairs.
Manuel Belgrano, a native of Buenos
Aires, returning from his studies in Eu-

rope, became interested in the commercial development of the colonies under the new code. He advanced from the idea of commercial freedom to the idea of political liberty, and was later accepted as a leader in the movement for emancipation. The commercial activity favoured by the code of 1778 helped to bring the colonies out of their isolation and increased their contact with other countries, thus opening them to the influx of ideas dominant in those countries. Awakening from their long period of stagnation, the colonists gradually conformed their activity to that of the more advanced nations. The movement under this new commercial freedom was revolutionary, since it enlarged colonial interests, and tended to encourage independent action. The reform initiated by Belgrano as secretary of the trade commission known as the *consulado* in 1794 brought owners of estates in the country into the *consulado*, and into coöperation

with the merchants. By this means a
new force was added to the movement
towards independence. The colonists
were brought into communication with
the outside world, not only commer-
cially but also intellectually. They
began to respond to influences from
abroad. The nearness of Venezuela to
the United States and to the West
Indies favoured the introduction of
books, under the less restricted inter-
course subsequent to 1797. This helped
to create an intellectual interest at
Caracas and some other parts of the
country (7). The French and North
Americans introduced a large number
of books, which, sold at low prices,
awakened a desire for reading, and
popularized among them many ideas
previously unknown. The English of
the Antilles exercised the same benefi-
cent influence, at first making light of
the legal prohibition, and after 1808
introduced books freely, thanks to the
alliance with Spain.

Nevertheless the influence of these imported books was immediately felt by only a limited class of cultivated persons in the countries in question, but it must be remembered that in all cases only a limited class has shaped the thinking of new republics. And the knowledge that Spain had assisted the rebellious British colonies in gaining their independence naturally weakened the argument that to rebel against the mother country was a crime.

In the early years of the revolutionary agitation many of the owners of European books kept them concealed in their houses. The Count of Ségur mentions a physician, whom he visited in Venezuela, who showed him the works of Rousseau and Raynal, which were usually hidden in a hollow beam, out of the reach of official inquirers.

To the other influences tending to render inefficient the laws prohibiting the importation of books there must be added the craving of the awakening secular mind for some other form of intellectual nourishment than that furnished by the church, whether through the curriculum of its schools or in the writings of the clergy. This hunger was not satisfied by the official correspondence which arrived from Spain nor by the desiccated items of the *Gaceta de Madrid,* nor even by the Spanish *Mercurio's* notes of births, deaths, and marriages within the horizon of the royal court. The smuggled books showed by the contrast they presented the extreme barrenness of the colonial existence, and aroused an intellectual revolt.

The influence of British North America was hardly less important than that proceeding from Europe. The successful struggle of the British colonies for independence, the effective organization of the United States, and the extraordinary progress of that country under its republican government awakened in the minds of the

Spanish colonists the ambition to lead their compatriots to a similar undertaking. This ambition was encouraged by the propaganda carried on by the citizens of the United States.

In spite of the governmental restrictions on the importation of books at the close of the colonial period, South America had a number of important collections. Two private libraries are notable for the influence they exerted on the early phases of the revolutionary movement. One of these libraries belonged to Antonio Nariño in Colombia, the other to José Antonio Rojas in Chile. The young creoles who gathered about Nariño, and drew inspiration from him and his books, initiated the revolution in the viceroyalty of New Granada. Rojas was in Europe during the years from 1772 to 1777, and he appears to have been an eager student of the liberal literature of the eighteenth century. He purchased and sent to America many of the more prominent works of that period. The *Encyclopédie* occupied a conspicuous place in his collection, and Raynal's *Philosophical history of European establishments and commerce in the Indies* excited his enthusiastic admiration. Martínez de Rozas, through his friendship with Rojas, had access to these books, and from them he acquired many of the ideas, which determined his career as one of the early leaders of the Chilean revolution.

A little later we find the Farewell Address of Washington and other addresses by the early American political leaders republished in translation in South American periodicals. The publication of these documents was a phase of the propaganda instituted to spread a knowledge of the principles of democracy as established in the United States.

The liberal ideas entertained by the younger creoles aroused violent opposition to the political doctrines introduced from the United States as one may see in the *Memoria sobre la revolución de Chile,* by Fray Melchor Martínez. These reflections illustrate not only the attitude of many ecclesiastics with respect to Spanish rule, but also reveal the distrust which increasing connection between the United States and the Spanish colonies awakened in the minds of conservative South Americans.

"The Boston republic," wrote Martínez, "isolated, and surrounded by many peoples desiring to imitate its ideas of liberty, recognizes and at the same time fears the weakness of its existence, and for this reason is making its greatest efforts to enlarge its boundaries and to extend its system, as the only method of providing for its stability and maintenance. To this end it puts into action all imaginable means, without hesitating at the most iniquitous and immoral, in order to attract the Spanish colonists to its depraved designs. The freedom of conscience and the freedom of the press assist it in publishing and spreading subversive and seditious principles and maxims, which always find reception with the majority of men, ruled by ignorance and malice. The clandestine trade and the permission to fish for whales introduce traders and adventurers from the United States into all the coasts, ports, islands, and other Spanish possessions, giving them opportunity to persuade the Spanish colonists of the flourishing state and advantageous situation of their country, decrying the Spanish Colonial government and subjection to the mother country in Europe as ignominious slavery. They magnify the riches and extent of these provinces; proclaim the injustice and tyranny with which the wealth is carried off to enrich Europe; describe the state of obscurity, abandonment, and civil nullity in which the colonists live; and offer with impudence all the aid of their great power to the peoples who may wish to shake off the yoke of legitimate and just government.

Moreover, they have adopted and put into execution the most powerful means to undermine and destroy the political and religious edifice of the Spanish colonies, sending clandestinely to all and each one of these possessions subjects for the purpose of establishing themselves and becoming citizens, with the design of perverting and destroying allegiance to the mother country " (8).

Friar Martínez affirms furthermore, that the Bostonese came as spies, married into the principal families, sought influence in the government, not embarrassed by the differences of religion, even becoming nominally Catholics as a means of acquiring freedom and security to advance themselves and to take an active part in seducing the inhabitants from their attachment to Spain.

Martínez was not an isolated objector to the advent of liberal ideas; he represented a party. An official report made to the president of Chile coupled Great Britain with the United States as a source of influence " for corrupting and perverting all these peoples, disposing and preparing them with its fallacious maxims to throw off the legitimate yoke of their ancient government, and of the true doctrine of the sacred and Catholic religion " (9).

The bitterness of the opposition to the liberal influences from foreign sources was indicated not only by documents in protest, but also later by the ferocity of some of the Spanish leaders in the war of independence. In the meantime, the creoles and mestizos, as an increasing party of opposition to Spanish rule, were animated by these influences to strengthen their opposition, and to adopt ideas proceeding from Great Britain and France, as well as some of the principles realized in the newly organized American government.

But the development of political liberalism encountered obstacles in the established traditions and practices of Spanish absolutism; and the practical conduct of affairs under an autocratic supreme government had much influence in maintaining a considerable part of the inhabitants loyal to that form of rule. Their positions under the government in Spain determined to a great extent their ideas. The viceroys, the governors, the *corregidores*, the judges of the audiencias, and the principal members of the clergy, as appointees of the crown, were inclined to be its loyal supporters. Charged with offices created by the king, the performance of their functions and their sense of responsibility made them inevitably advocates of the ideas underlying the organizations which they represented; and when forces beyond their control finally threatened to destroy the autocratic system, they were the last to modify their views in favour of a liberal régime.

The royal tradition of the seventeenth century still prevailed in the colonies as well as in Spain, which attributed to the kings of Spain, in spite of their mental and moral weakness, an exaggerated virtue and majesty, and saw in them a quality essentially divine. That was the age in which the unbounded conceit of Louis the Fourteenth led him to assert a close kinship between himself and God. The halo of divinity still blazed above the throne, and the people looked upon it with awe and honest reverence. The distance of the colonists from the royal presence magnified this sentiment, and created in them a mental predisposition, conscious or subconscious, to submit to a government imposed upon them without their counsel or consent; and the conservative force of this attitude of mind continued throughout the colonial period, even after they had begun to be irritated by the restrictions and abuses that limited their freedom and violated their sense of justice. Gradually, with the introduction of foreign ideas the colonists became aware of the existence of social conditions in other nations, quite different from those under which they were living, and to obtain for themselves similar conditions became in the course of time the aim and end of their activity.

The colonial mind, however, found it difficult to adapt itself to a purpose foreign to its experience. The movement suggested by imported ideas was a step forward in social progress, and this was a subject that had not been prominent within the early colonists' intellectual horizon. The dominance of the church in the society of the dependencies made the viewpoint of the clergy generally accepted. Whatever the exponents of religion asserted concerning progress was in general the colonists' opinion, and this opinion was, that what was held to be true yesterday ought to be regarded as true to-day. The *Index expurgatorius* is an illuminating commentary on this theory; it embraces within its list of condemned books a large number of serious and conscientious researches undertaken to enlarge the field of knowledge and thus to raise the standard of civilization. These researches it was foreseen would lead to conclusions that might supplant or modify affirmations unquestioned in the past.

The policy embodied in the *Index* was the policy adopted for the colonies by the government in Spain, and carried out by the governmental agencies in America. All the force of ecclesiastical and secular institutions was directed towards establishing and maintaining the pretensions of this policy in the public mind. Moreover, the colonists, in their long intellectual isolation, lacking scientific knowledge and the scientific spirit, had little or no appreciation of social advancement as exemplified in the exposition of scientific principles and their application in practical affairs, in which the modern mind sees the main features of progress.

All the political suggestion, whether from the United States, France, or Great Britain, that came to the colonists, when they faced the problem of emancipation, favoured realizing the democratic spirit in the new governments. But the field had not been prepared for democracy. The public mind, as already indicated, was, by its long subjection to autocratic rule, instinctively inclined to accept some form of monarchy. In colonial New England democracy was a normal growth in a sparse population, where the opportunity to appropriate land for cultivation fostered equality of material possessions, and where the government of the mother country made no effort to modify the natural course of social development. The self-government permitted by Great Britain and practiced by the colonists had prepared them for democracy. In the Spanish colonies of

South America, on the other hand, the sentiment in favour of democracy was the sentiment of a party in opposition to the established order, provoked by the abuses and injustice of the actual government. Against this government the creoles revolted, and, allying with themselves the mestizos and the more civilized Indians, formed a political party entertaining democratic principles. But the weakness of this party, as a supporter of democracy, was that it had had no experience with democracy and no democratic traditions; it was democratic only by intelligence, by resolution, not by instinct.

Even after the rise of the democratic opposition many of the leading colonists, although creoles, remained monarchists. They approved and supported the movement for emancipation, but in their view liberty did not mean democracy. Neither Bolívar nor San Martín wished to establish a democratic government for the liberated colonies. The

higher clergy, whatever their origin, remained true to the ecclesiastical traditions of absolutism and obedience.
With respect to social forms and governmental principles, the views of the
colonists presented a bewildering com-
plex, out of which it required a century
to evolve a consolidated and persistent
political opinion.

III

The spirit of
the creoles

The government in Spain aimed to establish and maintain in America such class distinctions as had existed in Europe. It created a nobility; it granted lands to certain Spaniards emigrating to its American possessions; it required from the grantee a feudal oath similar to that exacted from the king's vassals; to certain landholders it assigned Indians to be their dependents, serfs, or slaves; and it created a class of officials almost entirely composed of men sent from Spain. Besides these classes based on the king's favour, there were other classes recognized by their racial peculiarities or the countries of their origin. The Spaniards' habit of regarding the creoles as untrustworthy and inferior to themselves resulted in making the two groups assume the attitude towards one another which is ordinarily assumed by different peoples. The practice of ignoring the creole's claim to public office was not so much the result of a legal prohibition as the effect of a social prejudice directed against him (10).

The antagonism of the creoles and the Spaniards, the two classes the most nearly related to one another, was continually increasing. The creoles were vain and overbearing in their attitude towards the Europeans who arrived impoverished from Spain. Their vanity led them to refuse to work or to engage in trade, and to neglect to cultivate the estates they had inherited, while the Europeans took advantage of this state of things to acquire property and an enviable position in their several communities. Many of the Spaniards of humble origin after settling in America found no difficulty in allying themselves with families of distinction.

Their prosperity tended to inflame the hostility of the creoles, and to widen the breach between the two classes. In the course of time unfriendly relations between the creoles and the Europeans became intensified, and manifested themselves in the development of different political aspirations. The creoles became the advocates of liberty and emancipation, while the Europeans continued to support Spain's traditional colonial policy.

The progress of French arms in Spain, the loss of Aragón by the Spaniards, the occupation of Galicia and Estremadura by the French, and the various battles in which the French were victorious, dampened the spirits of the Spaniards in America. Dr. Juan Martínez de Rozas, a Chilean patriot, wrote in September, 1809, of Spain's prospects that he did not doubt for a moment that all was lost, and that for the malady there was no cure (11).

The creoles were interested in spread-

ing this view, as an argument in favour
of independence. A little later, in the
autumn of that year, two commissioners
arrived from Spain, charged by the
central junta to develop in the colonies
the sentiment of loyalty to the cause of
Spain. In this manner the two opposing ideas and purposes were brought into
immediate conflict. One of these commissioners, Antonio de Mendiburu, was
a brother of Rozas's wife, and his
activity as an advocate of the Spanish
cause was in a great measure destroyed by Rozas's dominance over him.
Recognizing this fact, his colleague,
Joaquín de Molina, reported to the central junta the unfortunate effect produced by Mendiburu's attitude; he also
called the attention of that body to the
existence in America of combustible
material that might produce a general
conflagration. The awakening spirit of
revolution in the colonies was hardly
appreciated in Spain. A pamphlet published in Sevilla, in 1808, aimed to dis-

sipate the notion that the colonists could be separated from Spain:

" They are our sons, our grandsons, our brothers, and our friends. We are of the same family, and in indissoluble domestic peace, we are convinced of our common interests. They will follow our fate if we are fortunate, and if we should be overwhelmed, they will be independent, and give us an asylum " (12).

The spirit of revolt was intensified by the prospect of French dominion in Spain, and by the knowledge that Napoleon was sending agents to America to secure the adhesion of the colonists to his plans. The colonists protested against the Napoleonic project and were not disposed to accept submission to Spain if it should be dominated by a foreign power. At the same time a sentiment of loyalty to the deposed King Ferdinand the Seventh was aroused in the colonies. Those persons who assumed this attitude magnified

Ferdinand's virtues and affirmed that he alone had the right to govern the colonies; they declared that it was the duty of Americans to remain faithful to him and to use whatever means they could command to restore him to the throne. Proclamations in manuscript were distributed among the people to stimulate resistance to the French and devotion to the king.

This attitude indicates that the colonists recognized that they were not subject to the government of Spain but to the king's personal authority. In this movement the clergy were especially zealous. " They thundered from the pulpits against the invaders of Spain calling them godless perjurers and monsters from hell. In these sermons, it was related that Napoleon and his soldiers profaned the churches, made a mockery of the worship, and administered the communion to their horses " (13).

A considerable impulse towards the

independence of the colonies was received from Spain. The royal power being in abeyance, the nation itself took up the task of preserving and reforming the national organization; in fact, of organizing the Spanish Empire as a single state. Local committees, or juntas, were formed, and a constituent congress was assembled. In this congress for the first time representatives of the colonies assumed the dignity and responsibility of participants in the organization and exercise of the national power. To this task they rose with great zeal and generosity. When, later, the mother country abandoned the ideal, in the service of which a liberal constitution for Spain, the famous Constitution of 1812, had been framed, the American members of the congress carried back to their respective colonies important information concerning methods of organizing for popular government. The local *juntas soberanas* in Spain naturally suggested the creation

of similar bodies in America, and only
the existence of these bodies was needed
to produce a state of things facilitating
the movement towards actual independence. The reversion of Spain to absolutism made more evident than ever before the difference between the point of
view of the colonies and that of the
mother country.

At this time Juan Martínez de Rozas
was admitted to membership in the
cabildo of Santiago. By his intelligence
and energy he exerted an important influence in spreading abroad more advanced ideas of independence among
the people. Already in 1808, the advocates of loyalty to the king began to
suspect that the colony was not entirely
of one mind touching that subject.
There were persons who held that in
case the French became masters of
Spain, the Chileans should reject all
domination which the Peninsula might
attempt to impose.

The suspected diversity of views appeared among the thirty-six members of the Chilean revolutionary congress, which was organized in 1810, and the controversies among the reactionary, moderate, and radical factions impeded the progress of an orderly revolution.

At this point Carrera came upon the scene. He was young, rich, talented, and well-born. He sought and obtained the privilege of addressing the congress. His fiery eloquence made even the sluggish members see visions, but their timidity and the burden of their traditions prevented them from moving forward to the promised land that was pointed out to them. The words of the young orator, however, found an echo in the hearts of the people. They and the soldiers were impressed by tales of his achievements in Europe, by his service in Spain against Napoleon, by his amiable conduct, by his insinuating speech, and by his generosity (14).

In Chuquisaca and in Quito the revolutionary spirit was early manifested in a vigorous opposition to the projects of France. In Quito the patriots formed a *junta de gobierno* after the Spanish model, and proposed that the administration of the province should be conducted in the name of Ferdinand the Seventh. The purpose here, as in other instances, was to create an organization that would enable them to resist the domination of Spain ruled by France, with the logical consequence that if Spain should remain subject to France the colony would become independent.

This was consistent with the view generally expressed by prominent patriots that, if the Spaniards acknowledged a new sovereign as a consequence of being subdued by a superior force, the colonists were under no obligation to accept that sovereign, since they had not been subdued. Under the colonial administration, it was the king and the council of the Indies who exercised supreme governmental authority over the colonies, and not the agencies constituting the government of Spain. Dr. Rozas, in his *Catecismo político cristiano*, refers to this subject:

" The inhabitants and provinces of America have sworn fidelity only to the kings of Spain, and were only vassals and dependents of those kings, as were and have been the inhabitants and provinces of the Peninsula. The inhabitants and provinces of America have not sworn fidelity to the inhabitants and provinces of Spain, nor are they their vassals. The inhabitants and provinces of Spain have, then, no authority, jurisdiction, or power over the inhabitants and provinces of America " (15).

The first meeting of the junta at Quito was held on the 25th of September, 1808; the presiding officer was Juan Pío Montúfar, Marquis of Selva Alegra. This organization was favoured by Andrés Rosillo, Frutos Joaquín Gutiérrez, Camillo Forres, José Gregorio Gutiérrez, José María del

Castillo Rada, and José Acevedo (16).
In the absence of facilities for printing, papers in manuscript were circu-
lated, advocating the projects of the
junta; but it was not until March,
1809, that knowledge of this enterprise
became public. Among these papers
were those called *Cartas de Suba* which
have been attributed to Frutos Joaquín
Gutiérrez (17).

The noteworthy botanical investiga-
tions by Mutis and his associates and
Caldas's studies in geography and
physics had excited the enthusiastic co-
operation of many of the cultivated
young creoles in New Granada, but the
rising tide of revolution turned their
attention to a new field of inquiry.
They ceased to be interested in researches in natural science; they directed their attention to political and
social questions. Antonio Nariño became especially conspicuous by printing
a Spanish translation of *Les droits de
l'homme*. In the group gathered about

him and deriving inspiration from
his extensive collection of books was
born the spirit of revolt and the desire
for the country's political independence.
Nariño was exiled for printing *The
rights of man* and imprisoned after
his return from Europe to New Granada. This limited his influence in developing the revolutionary spirit; in
fact the attitude which he assumed in
the elaborate document known as his
Defense indicates that immediately
after exile he was not willing to break
with the royal authority.

The sentiments in favour of revolution found a public and practical expression in the summer of 1810. The
most intelligent and distinguished members of New Granada creole society assembled in the great square of the
capital, on the 20th of July, and declared for independence (18). The
mental attitude of the persons engaged
in this movement was not definitely
fixed. The way to a compromise was

not yet closed. Here as in other provinces in the beginning of the revolt there were various courses that might possibly be taken. The claim to be acting in the name of Ferdinand the Seventh seemed to the timid or conservative a safe course. This might serve a purpose in the beginning, but it was hardly less reasonable than the later project to place Spanish princes at the head of such states as might be organized in the several viceroyalties or captaincies-general, after they had become independent. This attitude of mind was, however, completely changed after the arrival of the Spanish general Morillo at Bogotá, and it became known that he had determined to execute the leaders of the revolution. There was then no longer any possibility of a compromise. The only way out of the complicated situation was towards freedom and an independent government.

The part of J. M. Caballero's chronicle *En la independencia*, relating to the revolution in New Granada, forms a noteworthy account, especially of the local events of the period. The editors say of it:

" The *epopeya* of our independence, the dreadful days of Morillo, figure in all of our manuals of history, but perhaps in no writing are they seen with greater clearness and with so much richness of detail, as in this memorandum, where the patriot of Bogotá sets down the daily events. He is the eyewitness and actor in many of them. Speaking of the entrance of Viceroy Amar, for example, he says: ' I was a witness because I aided in serving the table ' " (19).

The spirit of the creoles in advocating the revolution manifested itself in the Spanish colonies by setting aside the restrictions on printing; by declaring the freedom of the press; by making provision for schools, where they had not existed, or where they had been abolished by the expulsion of the

Jesuits; and by increasing the facilities for the education of women. It aimed to have justice administered through a distinct department of government; to have the ports open to trade with other countries besides Spain; to remove the limitation previously imposed on certain forms of production; to abolish slavery and titles of nobility and to have all citizens regarded as equal before the law.

The absence of political extremists is noteworthy in the agitation for independence in the Spanish American colonies. " In periodicals and gazettes the necessity of conceding rights to the people with sobriety and with caution is insisted upon; it is affirmed that the authorities are the best judges of the degree of liberty which the citizen merits; and it was frequently proclaimed that the greatest enemies of America were not the Spaniards but exaggerated ideas " (20).

IV

The attitude of the Church

The first movement of revolutionary opinion not only concerned political affairs but also affected the relations of the individual citizen to religion. The drift towards political liberty encountered a government for the colonies organized in Spain and manned by officials sent with instructions from Madrid. In that government the colonists themselves had practically no participation. They were either indifferent to it or irritated by it. The colonists for the greater part held a very different attitude towards religion from that held towards the state. The church had impressed itself upon the minds of the people; it had persuaded them of an unending existence, and presenting terrible visions of the damned, had convinced them that only by its ministrations was it possible to escape from everlasting torment in hell. Revolt against the political administration seemed to offer glimpses of an earthly paradise, but persons in rebellion against the church were conceived to be exposed to the infernal horrors which the clerical imagination had pictured. It was natural, therefore, that after the first generous impulse towards all forms of liberty, the pendulum of religious sentiment and opinion should swing back to ecclesiastical orthodoxy. After Juan de Egaña had published his inquiries as to the desirability of freedom of worship in Chile, his adverse views found extensive acceptance beyond the limits of that province. His *Memoria política sobre si conviene en Chile la libertad de cultos* was republished in both Lima (1823) and Bogotá (1828). The editor of the edition published in Bogotá wrote:

"It is impossible to read this *Me-*

moria with attention and impartiality
without becoming fully convinced of
the three principal points which the
author demonstrates, and from which
results as a necessary corollary that the
liberty of worship is pernicious to the
health of the state; 1. that the multitude of religions in a single state
conduces to irreligion; 2. that the existence of two religions conduces to a
conflict likely to end with the destruction of the state, or of one of
the religious parties; 3. that the uni-
formity of religion is the most
effective means for establishing tranquillity in the affairs of the nation " (21).

The text of this work in the edition
of Bogotá consists of fifty pages; the
notes and additions cover one hundred
and twenty-two pages, the whole forming a not very enlightening volume of
religious controversy, yet proving to the
satisfaction of that writer the desirability of intolerance under the condi-

tions present in Chile and the other states of Spanish South America.

The mental attitude of the clergy towards the revolution varied with the varying aims of the revolutionists. When it was the revolutionists' purpose to adhere to Ferdinand the Seventh, the bulk of the clergy were zealous supporters of the plan; when revolution meant the rejection of the king and the creation of republics, the higher clergy found it impossible to renounce their allegiance to the sovereign.   They owed their appointments and promotion to him; their relation to him was immediate and personal; and they regarded themselves as agents charged with the execution of the sovereign's ecclesiastical policy in America.

Certain European statesmen believed that the conservatism of the clergy would make a secession of the colonies impossible.   Shortly after his return from America, the Count of Ségur was received by the Count of Vergennes, to whom he expressed the opinion that the Spanish colonies were drifting inevitably towards a revolt against Spanish rule. Vergennes did not share this view, but believed that a revolution was made impossible " by the ignorance of the inhabitants of the great colonies and by the power of the clergy " (22).

The conservative clergy did indeed exercise a powerful influence over a large number of ignorant persons, but in spite of inadequate schools and the restriction and limited importation of books, a considerable minority of the inhabitants acquired knowledge and a certain degree of intellectual development; and here, as in other instances, the minority brought about the revolution.

The church acquired vast amounts of property in lands and buildings during the colonial period, and this great aggregation of wealth in the hands of the church aroused the hostility of the revolutionists; it made them disposed to include ecclesiastical affairs in their general program of reform. The revolutionary sentiment in opposition to the Inquisition and the accumulation of property by the church is illustrated by Monteagudo's address at the inauguration of the Patriotic Society of Buenos Aires. He charged the church with " raising the standard of the cross in order to assassinate men with impunity; to introduce discord among them; to deprive them of their rights; and to snatch from them the wealth which they possess in the soil of their country "(23).

Time has dimmed the world's memory of the Inquisition, but when the colonists looked forward to independence its deeds were not a faded vision. Whatever mistakes the revolutionists may have made in carrying out reforms, the early abolition of the Inquisition was surely not one of them. That institution had spread a blight over the intellectual life of the colonies; it had smothered the spirit of inquiry; it had silenced the voice of reason; and under its malign influence Christian charity disappeared. It pretended to interpret minds of which its agents had no adequate comprehension. It developed in its service characters not greatly unlike those which its own traditions describe as denizens of hell. It is to the credit of the political reformers that they saw in the complete destruction of the Inquisition the first essential step towards individual liberty and social progress.

The tradition of the church and the relation of the principal ecclesiastics to the government in Spain furnished to certain persons a more or less reasonable ground of opposition to the revolution. These were especially those members of the clergy whose exalted position brought them into close association with the higher governmental officials; but when the course of the revolution appeared to lead directly to independence a reasonable regard for their worldly well-being suggested to a considerable number of ecclesiastics a manifestation of sympathy with the party that was destined to exercise power in the new state. It could not, however, be expected that the highest officials of the church would consent to follow meekly a course which worldly interest and common sense might dictate. Instead, therefore, of submission of this character, there appeared at Tunja in New Granada, in 1813, a periodical called *El Argos*, designed to defend persons who had been regarded as enemies of the republic. The effect of this defense was to stir up a controversy and provoke a debate on the relation of the clergy to the movement for independence. A feature of this controversy is seen in the archbishop's declaration against Bolívar after the general's arrival in New Granada and the subsequent protest of the republican government against the archbishop's edict (24).

However much the patriots may have been disposed to criticize the church as it was conducted during the colonial period their religious instinct remained essentially unimpaired. There was only needed an event that seemed to indicate the favour of heaven to awaken the spirit of worship. The battle of Boyacá, the destruction of the royalist forces, and Bolívar's arrival at Bogotá constituted such an event or series of events. Therefore after the tumultuous flight of the royalists from the capital, the patriots who remained crowded about the Christian altars to assist at the *Te Deum*, giving thanks for divine deliverance from the tyranny and cruelties of an enraged enemy.

Even the superstition displayed by the Spaniards provoked no protest from many persons, whether royalists or patriots. When, for instance, Caracas was destroyed by an earthquake, the

event was announced as a manifestation
of God's wrath called forth by the
fact that Venezuela had dared to revolt
against Spain. The bulk of all parties
accepted this utterance as consistent with
their religious views. In spite of the
movement towards liberty the great
body of the worshipers had not perma-
nently laid aside any of their supersti-
tions. When a canon of the cathedral
of Buenos Aires was stricken with
paralysis, the affliction was held to be a
divine punishment for his espousing the
cause of emancipation (25).

Not only earthquakes and sudden
death were regarded as instances of
divine punishment inflicted for sin, but
other events also fell into the same cate-
gory; the piracy of Drake, diseases re-
sulting from unsanitary conditions, and
numerous other ills appeared as imposed
directly by divine decree. Wanting
scientific knowledge, the scientific spirit,
and even freedom for scientific inquiry,
the colonists were disposed to explain

many observed phenomena by a method not greatly unlike that employed by primitive man. A very considerable part of the population remaining in this state was naturally slow to put faith in any human means for improving its physical condition or the evils incident to man's relation to nature. For such persons the project of the revolutionists was an idle dream, or a criminal undertaking against a long-existing and divinely approved order of things.

There were, however, certain ecclesiastics who departed from the straight and narrow way of religious conservatism; some, like Camilo Henríquez, the editor of *La Aurora*, became bright and shining lights of the revolution; their superior learning made it possible for them to render important services in the cause of liberty.

Regarding slavery, the ecclesiastics were generally rather in sympathy with the ideas of the revolutionists than with the plans and practices of the old régime. From the beginning the revolutionists had aimed at the abolition of Indian slavery, and the majority of the clergy were ready to accept this view. Some of the religious orders, it is true, owned slaves, but these owners were generally more humane and generous than other classes in their views concerning the treatment of slaves, and they were among the first to free them. In the long wars between the Spanish and the Indians, it was the members of the clergy especially who stood for conciliation and for establishing satisfactory relations between the two peoples; and this spirit gained force among them when it was observed that a large secular party had gathered about the standard of individual liberty and national independence.

While the ecclesiastics were willing to release the Indians from physical bondage, they had no mind to accord them freedom of spirit; they attacked the Indian's ancient religious traditions, and proposed to transform that element of his nature which was most uncompromising. They were willing to make him physically free, but determined to recast his mind in a new and rigid mould.

A noteworthy feature of the opposition between the ecclesiastics and the political liberals was the storm that raged in New Granada over the Freemasons conceived as representing liberal or anti-clerical views. This took the form of a literary controversy, in which conflicting opinions were set forth in a flood of papers and pamphlets. Some of these were *El Perro de Santo Domingo, Guerras fanáticas contra masones, Verdadero censor de Colombia, El Gallo antimason.* An especially vigorous defender of the Masons was *El Soldado de Colombia.* This discussion may have aroused intellectually many persons not hitherto greatly interested in the larger public questions made prominent by the revolution; and it

widened the breach between the liberal
advocates of the revolution and the conservative, or ecclesiastical party. The
leading ecclesiastics declaimed vigorously against the Masons from their
pulpits, and their authority as priests
helped to keep alive the controversy.

The opposition to the Masons which
found expression in numerous publications stimulated the spirit of intolerance,
and provoked hostility to all projects to
recognize any form of worship but the
Catholic one. An utterance which became famous in this controversy was
Padre Ruiz's *La Tapa del Congola*.
The historian Groot notes the fact that
Ruiz has become immortal, since, when
it is desired to characterize a rough and
unpolished piece of writing, it is said
to be *La Tapa del Congola* (26).

Santander's little periodical, *El
Patriota*, announced that to discuss
Freemasonry was then the mode.
" Common folks," it said, " women and
hypocrites believe that freemasonry is

something from the other world, a diabolical invention and a school of vice.
Cultivated persons laugh at such sup-
positions, and there are among them
even valiant apologists of the institution." The rest of the article was de-
signedly humorous, but it is clear that
the general attitude of the writer was
not hostile to the Freemasons. A
month later, appeared a paper, or pamphlet, antagonistic to Freemasonry,
called *El Gallo de San Pedro*, written
by the presbyter Francisco Margales. It
reproduced opinions opposed to the
Freemasons, extracted from various
European publications, and it is an in-
dication of a strong support of these
opinions by a large class of the inhabitants. In two days, eight hundred
copies of the paper were sold, and the
demand from the provinces was such as
to require a large new edition. This
showed a widespread opposition to the
Masonic lodges in Colombia and was
the beginning of an abundant issue of

papers and pamphlets, making evident
that the inhabitants were fast becoming
emancipated from the intellectual re-
straint imposed by the politico-eccle-
siastical administration of the colonies
(27).

Some of the ecclesiastics were not
disposed to approve the government's
action in limiting the freedom which
the church had previously enjoyed. In
1821 Archbishop Bartolomé of Lima
found that his official conscience was
opposed to certain orders of the government in closing religious houses; and
for expressing this opposition he was
expelled from the country. His objec-
tion, however, appears not to have been
founded on a belief that the authority
of the new government was transitory;
for before he left Lima on the 5th of
September, 1826, he wrote to Lord
Cochrane:

" I am convinced that the independence of this country is sealed forever;
I shall express this opinion to the Span-

ish government and to the Holy See;
at the same time I shall do whatever I
can to overcome their obstinacy, to
maintain the tranquillity, and to
favour the wishes of the inhabitants of America which I greatly
appreciate " (28).

Clerical antagonism to the new government was sometimes carried to extremes. In a periodical called *El Mon-
talbán,* edited and published by Padre
Padilla, certain liberal articles appear-
ing in *La Bagatela* were denounced as
" hostile to religion " and even as
" immoral ". The author of these articles was charged with attempting to
make the clergy odious in the eyes of
the people. To these accusations *La
Bagatela* replied that the attacks were
not directed against the clergy in general but against the evils and abuses of
the church (29). With this good beginning the debate went on, displaying
the usual amenities of a religious controversy. A little later the *Gaceta*

ministerial de Cundinamarca entered the lists on the side of *La Bagatela*.

Later the controversy assumed an even more important character. In the early part of his term as vice president Nariño addressed the congress, offering to present his draft of a constitution for the republic. His letter to the congress on this subject was dated at Rosario de Cúcuta, May 20th, 1821. When the legislative commission, to whom Nariño's draft had been referred, laid the constitution before the congress, it was found to contain no article making the Catholic, Apostolic, and Roman religion the religion of the state. Some of the representatives wished to insert such an article, but this project encountered the opposition of the majority, whereupon a member of the minority provoked a noisy scene in the congress when that body had assembled to sign the document. This was on the 5th of September, 1821. The session was continued the following day, when the case

of the offending member was disposed
of by expelling him from the congress.

On the eve of the congress of 1823
conflicting opinions were revived concerning various religious questions. It
was proposed to introduce an article into
the constitution providing that the Roman Catholic religion should be dominant in the republic, and that no other
creed should be tolerated. Two periodicals, *El Insurgente*, attributed to
General Nariño, and *El Correo* partici-
pated in this controversy (30). *El
Correo* was fertile in its mockery of
Dr. Manuel Baños, the noisy advocate
of Catholicism, who had been expelled
from the preceding congress, and who
now rejoiced in his reëlection as a
representative of Tunja. The editors
hailed him as a representative with instructions from Torquemada requiring
him to reëstablish the Inquisition and
burn the works of Vatel, Bentham,
Constant, and Van-Espen, and to sub-
stitute for them Torrubias, Fray Luis

de Granada, and Larraga.   The extremists among the clergy and their
supporters were so thoroughly convinced
that their doctrines embraced the whole
truth that they were unable to see in
any other religious view a valid claim
for recognition.

V

Monteagudo and the periodicals of Buenos Aires

The most noteworthy periodicals issued at Buenos Aires in the first decade of the nineteenth century were the *Telégrafo mercantil*, the *Semanario de agricultura*, the *Gaceta de Buenos Aires*, and the *Correo de comercio*. The *Telégrafo mercantil* was edited and published by Francisco Antonio Cabildo. Its brief career extended from April 1st, 1801 to October 17th, 1802. It was designed to occupy in Buenos Aires a place similar to that occupied by the *Mercurio peruano* in Lima, but it failed in this design through the lack of a group of contributors equal to those who gave to the Peruvian periodical its superior character. The *Semanario de agricultura* was edited by Juan Hipólito Vieytes, and ran from September 1st, 1802, until February 11th, 1807 (31).

Both of the other periodicals mentioned were founded in 1810, and their character was in a large measure affected by the revolutionary agitation which culminated in that year. The most prominent writer of the *Gaceta* was Bernardo Monteagudo, who was an especially eloquent expounder of revolutionary doctrine. He had, moreover, great capacity for making enemies even among the advocates of reform. He had received the title of Doctor from the University of Chuquisaca, and in the dissertation presented by him on that occasion there is reflected the royalist instruction which then prevailed at the University. He had apparently a passing vision of kingly majesty, of the monarch peacefully and securely seated on his throne amidst the splendours associated with his exalted position, the source of public order, the especially brilliant star in the

social firmament, the image of God on
earth (32). The change in his views
may be seen in the fact that in 1809,
two or three years later, he was an
active participant in the unsuccessful
revolution at Chuquisaca. After the
suppression of that outbreak he was
confined for a short time in the prison
of the audiencia of that city (33).
Later he was engaged in the revolutionary movement at Potosí. This uprising was not more successful than the
revolt at Chuquisaca, and Monteagudo,
soon after this event, appeared in
Buenos Aires, where almost immediately he became noted as a writer advocating revolution. His first article appeared in the *Gaceta de Buenos Aires*.
That periodical was usually issued twice
a week. At first Monteagudo edited
one of the two issues, while Vicente
Pazos Silva edited the other, but later
both numbers were edited by Monteagudo. On leaving the *Gaceta de
Buenos Aires* Monteagudo founded *El*

Mártir ó Libre. This periodical ran
its brief course from March 29th to
May 25th, 1812. Its early suspension
was due to lack of public support.
Another periodical founded at Buenos
Aires by Monteagudo on January 10th,
1815, was called *El Independiente.*

The bulk of Monteagudo's early
writings appeared in these three periodicals. As a brilliant young creole of
twenty-five or twenty-six years, well
educated, bearing from the University
the title of Doctor, noted for the part
he had played in the revolution of
1809, he enjoyed marked prestige
among the youth of Buenos Aires. His
energy and his eloquence attracted them
to his cause; but the vigour of his active
mind subjected him constantly to the
danger of going to extremes. His lack
of political experience and his limited
knowledge of practical affairs gave to
his utterances an academic or theoretical
quality. This is particularly true of
what he wrote during the five or six

years of his residence in Buenos Aires. In this early period he emphasized the necessity of returning to the primitive virtues as a condition of successful democracy. "To arrive at the sanctuary of liberty," he wrote, "one must pass through the temple of virtue. Liberty is not achieved by insulting satire, or simple discourse. One must not do violence to the rights of man if one would form a constitution that will guarantee those rights" (34).

A zealous revolutionist, Monteagudo held that "all human institutions stand or fall according as impartiality and justice more or less rule in their spirit" (35). He maintained vigorously the equality of all men before the law (36). He made it clear, however, that this applied to active citizens, recognizing that there were two classes of persons among the inhabitants who were not active citizens, namely aliens, and natives who had not acquired political rights (37).

In these early years Monteagudo appears to have accepted the doctrine of a social contract. " Between men and the law," he wrote, " between the sovereign and the citizen, between the constitution and the people there is a reciprocal pact, or contract, by which all are obliged to preserve and maintain themselves within the precise limits designated by necessity at the time of the convention " (38).

It followed from this relation of the people to the holders of political authority, that independence is " a principle sanctioned by nature and solemnly recognized by the great council of impartial nations " (39). " It would be an insult to the American people to admit the necessity of proving that we ought to be independent " (40). " We are free because we desire and are able to be free; it is the order of nature, and yet we are treated as rebels. The enemy of liberty and humanity is the real rebel; he is the horrible monster on which public authority everywhere ought to set its mark " (41).

Like the majority of the leading revolutionists, Monteagudo on many occasions emphasized the thought that popular education was an essential element in the basis of a free state. " Ignorance," he said, " is the firmest support of despotism, and the only way to destroy despotism is to dissipate ignorance " (42).

" Down to the end of the eighteenth century Spain needed no other force in order to maintain the colonial system than the superstition and ignorance of the people " (43).

Monteagudo returned to this theme later, " Enlightenment gives man power to dominate himself and in a certain measure to dominate nature; it causes to disappear the awful phantom of chance, to which the thoughtless attribute the greater part of their misfortunes." The spread of enlightenment he found, moreover, to be the most effective means for reducing crime in society, since crimes are "only practical errors, for no one becomes a delinquent except through a false calculation" (44).

Monteagudo's conception of the kind of knowledge needed to supplant the ignorance prevailing in the colonies is indicated by his statement that in every nation the science of politics is especially necessary; it is through it that states are founded, and on it depends their prosperity and maintenance (45). At the same time he recognized the futility and even the danger of mere preaching and the constant utterance of platitudes, for, "the heart of a people becomes hardened by hearing maxims, words, and precepts repeated, which do not go beyond mere theories, and which have no support, even in the conduct of public functionaries" (46).

Monteagudo's views of the limitations of suffrage were set forth in the

Gaceta de Buenos Aires, February 14th, 1812. " Every man over twenty years of age," he wrote, " who is not under the domination of any other person or has not been made infamous by a public crime fully proved and recorded; who knows how to read and write and exercises a profession, of any kind whatever, provided that he causes himself to be inscribed in the civil register of his canton after having lived more than a year in the territory of the United Provinces, subjecting his person and property to the fulfilment of the obligations that are imposed upon him, shall enjoy the right of active citizenship " (47).

Monteagudo's political views made him a partisan of Carlos María Alvear (48) and his advocacy contributed in some measure to the general's elevation in January, 1815, to the position of Supreme Director of the Argentine State. When Alvear was overthrown the leaders of his party found it for

their interest to withdraw from the
country. This was the occasion of
Monteagudo's going into exile in
1815 (49). His residence in France
where monarchy had acquired general
prestige through the Congress of Vienna
induced him to advocate constitutional
monarchy as a form of government
suited to the states to be formed in the
revolting Spanish colonies in South
America, instead of a democratic commonwealth administered by a dictator
appointed for a specified period.

On going into exile Monteagudo's
contributions to the periodicals of
Buenos Aires ceased. His later activity
in the cause of independence was in
association with San Martín in Chile
and Perú.

VI

Camilo
Henríquez
and La
Aurora de
Chile

Santiago de Chile gave public voice
to revolutionary doctrines a little later
than Buenos Aires. The medium of
this utterance was *La Aurora de Chile*
(1812–1813), the first periodical published in that dependency. Earlier
printing in Chile was limited to isolated
sheets and a few small pamphlets issued
in the last quarter of the eighteenth
century. In 1789 the *cabildo* of Santiago petitioned the king for permission
to establish a printing press, but without any satisfactory result. In 1810
Matthew Arnold Hœrvel, a Swede,
naturalized in the United States, arrived
in Chile, and was commissioned by the
government to introduce into the
country a battery of artillery and a
printing press. The press arrived at

Valparaíso on the American frigate *Galloway* the 24th of November, 1811, and was transported to Santiago, where it was received by the government and installed in the ancient building of the *Universidad de San Felipe*. With the press arrived three printers from the United States, Samuel Burr Johnston, William H. Burdige, and Simon Garrison. Under a decree of February 1st, 1812, these men were employed by the government, with an annual salary of one thousand pesos each. Already the government had sought an editor "endowed with political principles, with religion and talent, and, besides, with natural and civil virtues", and appointed to that position Fray Camilo Henríquez, with a salary of six hundred pesos a year.

The first number of *La Aurora* appeared on the 13th of February, 1812. A contemporary writer says, "It is not possible to exaggerate the joy caused by the periodical's establishment. Men ran through the streets with a copy of it in their hands, stopping whomsoever they met, read and reread its contents, congratulating themselves on their great good-fortune and promising themselves that by this means the ignorance and blindness in which they had hitherto lived would be banished and would be followed by enlightenment and culture, which would transform Chile into a kingdom of savants " (50).

Whatever favourable expectations the royalist party may have derived from the motto of the prospectus, *Viva la Unión, la Patria y el Rey*, or from any other source, were dissipated by the political doctrine set forth in the first number of *La Aurora*, affirming the right of all peoples to provide for themselves such a government as would be best suited to them. " It is one of the rights of the people to reform the constitution of the state. In fact, the constitution ought to be adapted to the actual circumstances and necessities; as the circumstances vary, the constitution should be changed. There is no law, no custom that ought to remain fixed if from it proceeds a detriment, an inconvenience, a disturbance of the body politic " (51).

The positive revolutionary doctrine announced by Henríquez in the early numbers of *La Aurora* induced the provisional government of Chile to seek to control the editor's statements, but this only served to irritate him. He refused to publish the governmental decree, but in reply printed an extensive extract from Milton's discourse on the freedom of the press. After this reproof, Henríquez's utterances became more uncompromising in their advocacy of a complete change in the form of government. To the royalists the attitude of *La Aurora* appeared scandalous, and called forth pamphlets in defense of the viceregal régime. The fact that his shafts had penetrated the armour of his opponents stimulated him to improve his already effective propaganda.

Concerning the mental equipment of Camilo Henríquez, Cifuentes wrote that his erudition might not be profound, but it was extensive — an extensiveness which it is impossible not to admire, even to-day, if one thinks of the difficulty with which he had to contend in acquiring it. He wrote with equal facility on the most varied topics: constitutional law, political economy, public instruction, statistics, colonization, politics, industry, commerce, and, in general, on whatever subjects might interest the government and the public in their common task of organizing an independent state (52).

Compared with a modern weekly periodical, *La Aurora* presented only a limited list of topics. Each number contained usually an article of considerable length by the editor, with a few items of news, and an important quotation or two from a foreign source.

Among these quotations appeared a
Fourth of July address delivered in
Washington, a speech in the British
parliament, an address by President
Madison to the Senate, and Washington's Farewell Address. From time
to time there were published also
official documents issued either by Chile
or by some other of the provinces
in rebellion. But the most important
feature of the periodical was the articles
by the editor, Camilo Henríquez.
These articles contained not only com-
ments on the affairs of the revolution,
but also formed an appeal to the people
to stand by the cause of emancipation.

Under the title, *A Memorable
example*, Henríquez wrote:

" When England declared Boston
blockaded and began to oppress the city
with all her power, the minds of the
people became inflamed and the outcry
of religion reënforced that of liberty.
The churches resounded with energetic
exhortations against the oppressor.

These discourses produced a great effect.
When the people invoked heaven
against the oppressor, they did not delay
in rushing to arms. The rest of the
colony became more closely united with
the capital, all resolved to bury themselves under the ruins of their country
rather than to sacrifice their rights.
The sentiments of the men of all the
provinces were aroused in proportion to
the increase of Boston's misfortunes "
(53).

An editorial on the love of liberty
appeared July 23rd, 1812. After
citing notable examples of resistance to
tyranny, the writer closed with the following paragraph, which illustrates his
style and indicates his exalted sentiments:

" In the American provinces formerly subject to the Spanish empire,
a brilliant scene is opened at present.
The valour, the resolution of the heroes,
the enthusiasm of the ancient and
modern republicans have been displayed

gloriously for the great cause of national liberty. The sword of expiring tyranny has immolated in some places many victims; but from their blood new heroes have arisen. The genius of liberty presents in these regions a terrible and threatening countenance: undaunted courage and confidence fill the hearts of the patriots; terror and remorse oppress the hearts of the tyrants. The cruelties with which the ancient domination takes leave of the New World, its desperation and bloody fury, even in its latest breath, have made it more odious, have revealed completely its character, have placed men under the necessity of either conquering or dying. Moreover, the American revolution is like all revolutions with respect to the movements it inspires in the mind: the public enthusiasm, the new order of things, continues to reveal unknown talents and extraordinary men. The patriotic fire burns with greater facility and makes its presence more readily manifest in inflammable youth. Youth is the age of energy, of vigour, and of magnanimity. It is capable of great passions, it is also capable of great virtues and high purposes. In revolutions the spirit is exalted, heroes appear, and occupy the place that belongs to them. In revolutions are manifest those immortal deeds, those examples of generosity, the admiration of future ages " (54).

Throughout the fifty-eight numbers, the articles by Henríquez remain the most striking feature of the publication. They constitute a medley of patriotic exhortations, illustrative narration, and social philosophy, set forth in a style not infrequently assumed by the preachers of a new political gospel. Daring and uncompromising, the writer appears to be conscious of being the first to sound, without a faltering note, the trumpet call to stand for liberty and independence. By his translations of addresses by Washington, Thomas

Jefferson, and other champions of republicanism, he shows that what he demands for the Spanish colonies is in harmony with the most characteristic purpose of his age, the purpose most clearly conceived and most completely attained by the colonies of North America in their revolt against British domination. It was from the doctrines of British liberalism and the announced aims of the British colonies, rather than from the theories of the French revolution, that Henríquez drew his inspiration. Nevertheless the number of *La Aurora* next to the last contained a Spanish translation of Raynal's letter to the French National Assembly, which was read in that body March 31st, 1791.

Both in his prose articles and in his verses Henríquez displays a fiery patriotic zeal and the skill of an astute propagandist; and through his efforts *La Aurora* became the most notable early periodical advocating colonial independence.

The last number of *La Aurora* appeared on the 1st day of April, 1813;
it was immediately succeeded by *El
Monitor araucano;* this periodical was
edited in the beginning by Henríquez;
it became the official organ of the provisional government, and continued the
revolutionary propaganda that had been
carried on through the columns of *La
Aurora.* The work of printing *La
Aurora* was performed by the three
American printers, Johnston, Garrison,
and Burdige, for the first twenty-one
numbers; their work was temporarily
interrupted by the death of Burdige
and the brief imprisonment of Johnston and Garrison for participation in
a row in connection with the American consul's celebration of the Fourth
of July. The publication of the periodical was continued during this
interval by the efforts of José
Camilo Gallardo, who had had a limited experience in printing on a very
small scale some years earlier, and

who was later one of the Chileans trained in the art of printing by the Americans.

In the last days of 1813, the press
passed by lease under the control of
Gallardo on account of the departure of
Johnston. Garrison also abandoned his
trade as printer; unlike his companion,
he remained in Chile, and became a
merchant in Santiago. Matthew Arnold
Hœrvel, who, as agent of the government, had brought the printing press
from the United States, died at Valparaíso in 1819, after a life of alter-
nate prosperity and adversity, during
which he was successively, in Chile,
merchant, consular agent, captain of
militia, political exile on the island
of Juan Fernández, governor-intendant
of the province of Santiago, general
superintendent of police of Chile,
journalist, treasurer of the navy, and
official interpreter to the governor of
Valparaíso.

After his retirement from his early

enterprises, Henríquez continued to
serve the cause of independence, both
by his writings and by his practical participation in the work undertaken by the
Chilean congress.

VII

The internal dissension in Chile caused the main purpose of the revolution to pass momentarily from the public mind, and political discussion was for the time being suppressed by the domination of the royalists; but San Martín's passage of the Andes and the victories of Chacabuco and Maipú finally established Chilean independence and provoked discussion of a constitution for the new state. At this time San Martín was preparing to invade Perú, and to complete the emancipation of the Spanish colonies in South America.

Monteagudo as minister of Perú

At this point Monteagudo reappeared on the political scene. After his return from Europe, he went to Chile, and became *auditor de guerra* and interested in San Martín's plans. Later he was exiled to the province of Cuyo, and ordered to reside at San Luis. His active and ambitious spirit contemplated with extreme dissatisfaction the prospect of residing in that desert village. Two days after his arrival, he wrote to the Director of Chile, asking that he might be sent with a commission, even a subordinate one, to Europe or to the United States. He viewed with equal aversion isolation and associations with the royalist prisoners of war sent thither after the battles of Chacabuco and Maipú (55). The supposition that his banishment on this occasion was a consequence of a request made to the Chilean government by Pueyrredón, Director of Buenos Aires, gives an air of reasonableness to his petition for a commission. The Chilean authorities wished to retain his allegiance and feared his political influence. This is shown by Antonio José de Irisarri's letter to O'Higgins after the writer's interview with the exile. " In Buenos Aires," he wrote, " I am going to see if they will not send him to Europe as Gómez's secretary, a thing which he greatly desires; for I am persuaded that such a man as he is, ought not to be kept discontented among us, since we are still in revolution and nothing is impossible." Irisarri affirmed that Monteagudo might serve them far from Chile, and that he ought to be kept in their interest, even suggesting that they ought " to observe the wise maxim ' to devote a candle to God that he might confer favours, and one to the devil that he might do them no harm ' " (56).

Having returned from Cuyo, Monteagudo founded in Santiago a periodical called *El Censor de la revolución*. The first number appeared April 30th, 1820. It contained Monteagudo's article entitled *El siglo XIX y la revolución*. This according to Pelliza, his biographer, gave evidence of very notable intellectual progress on the part of the writer, of an increase in knowledge acquired during his residence in Europe; and of a marked development in the sobriety and force of his style. In July 1820, he published another article entitled *Estado actual de la revolución.* Only seven numbers of *El Censor* were issued. These, however, by reason of the writer's relation to San Martín and the army became in some sense a proclamation designed to spread liberal ideas in Perú, and to awaken the spirit of independence in those who still venerated the Spanish flag (57).

Bolívar's successful campaigns in Venezuela and New Granada, and San Martín's overthrow of the royalists in Chile left Perú as the principal region of the unsubdued. To convert Perú was the remaining great problem of the revolution. While San Martín was preparing to invade that country, Monteagudo was directing to the inhabitants his forceful propaganda.   His description of the state of the revolution published in *El Censor* was evidently not designed merely for the Chileans.   He wished the Peruvians to know how firmly and closely the lines were drawn about them.

Lima had been the political and social capital of the Spanish dependencies in South America.   Into it the mines had poured their enormous wealth.   Here were gathered the titled and untitled aristocracy, and the richest and proudest of the Spaniards resident in America gave to the society of the city an uncompromising   royalist   opinion,   and when it became evident that the leaders of this community were not disposed to accept the views and plans of the revolutionists there remained only the argument of force.   This San Martín presented   in   his   expeditionary   army from Chile.   He took possession of the city and established there a provisional government for Perú.   He assumed the headship of the administration with the title of Supreme Protector.

In the provisional government Monteagudo became the minister of war and of the navy. With General San Martín in command of the forces and Admiral Cochrane in command of the fleet, Monteagudo as minister of war and of the navy had little scope for his activity. The two other ministers were Juan García del Río, of government and foreign affairs, and Hipólito Unánue, of the treasury. After Monteagudo's arrival in Perú, he edited a periodical called the *Boletín del ejército*, but, after the organization of the civil government, it was superseded by *El Pacificador del Perú*. Like many of the other periodicals of the time, it had a brief existence, only lasting from April 10th to September 1st, 1821. In it appeared a noteworthy contribution to the revolutionary literature, setting forth the advantages of peace for both parties. *El Pacifica-*

dor expressed the ideas of the Supreme
Protector and his energetic minister;
and was thus a champion of aristocracy
and monarchy. The triumph of monarchy in Europe, as already indicated,
had greatly influenced Monteagudo.
Rivadavia, Belgrano, Sarratea, and Va-
lentín Gómez shared his views and regarded monarchy as the only possible
government for their country. This
appeared to them a natural conclusion,
since the revival of monarchy seemed to
relegate republicanism to the simple
society of Switzerland. On account of
their views Monteagudo and San
Martín found special favour in the
sight of the Peruvian nobles and re-
actionaries. These ideas, however,
aroused a bitter opposition among the
liberals, and here the parties began an
exciting conflict (58). García del Río
was positive on the side of the monarchists, but Unánue, of the treasury,
was passive, or more or less indifferent
in the controversy. On January 1st,

1822, Monteagudo was transferred
from the ministry of war and of the
navy to the ministry of government and
foreign affairs succeeding García del
Río (59). As minister of war and of
the navy, Monteagudo had issued decrees abolishing the *mita* and the pay-
ment of tribute by the Indians, emanci-
pating the slaves, creating schools,
founding the library of Lima (60), and
establishing courts of justice. Some of
his other acts present a less favourable
view of his administration, yet the
severity of his treatment of certain
Spaniards domiciled in Lima was in a
measure extenuated by their irreconcil-
able attitude.

VIII

The *Sociedad patriótica de Lima,* *La Sociedad* *patriótica* *de Lima* established through. the influence of Monteagudo, in the form of a literary association, served as a field for debate and as an agency for propagating political doctrines. Only a minority of the members were republicans, but the republicans as well as the advocates of monarchy expected that the discussions would contribute to the spread of their opinions.

On the 10th of January, 1822, San Martín, the Supreme Protector, announced by a decree his approval of this association.

The preamble to the constitution of the society declared that public instruction was the first need of society; that the government, failing to encourage it, commits a crime which the remotest posterity will have a right to avenge, and to curse its memory; that the general ignorance in which the Spanish government has kept America has been a tremendous act of tyranny; and that it was time to begin to redeem the people from this outrage. It announced, furthermore, that one of the means proposed to attain this end was the formation of a Patriotic Society, composed of the most distinguished men, united under the protection of the government, for discussing matters that might influence the institutions of the country in the best manner possible.

The constitution provided that the society should be composed of forty members, at first appointed by the government, and subsequently elected by the society. The meetings were required to be held, Tuesday and Friday of each week, in one of the halls or rooms of the university, and to be open

to the public. It was required that the
president of the society should be the
secretary of state.

" The object of the society," to quote
the eighth article of the constitution,
" is to discuss questions that may have
a direct or an indirect influence on the
public welfare, whether political, economic, or scientific subjects, without
any other restriction than that no attack
should be made on the fundamental
laws of the country, or the honour of
any citizen."

The preliminary meeting of the
charter members was held on the 20th
of January, 1822, in the reception hall
of the university. The president was,
as provided by the constitution, the
secretary of state, Colonel Bernardo
Monteagudo. Dr. Hipólito Unánue,
the secretary of the treasury, was elected
vice president. The inaugural address
of the president was delivered at the
next meeting, on the 12th of February.
This meeting, like the others, was held

in one of the halls of the University of San Marcos. The members being assembled, the bells announced at half past four that San Martín was approaching, and all the members went out to receive him. The principal event of this meeting was the delivery of Monteagudo's address.

The theme of this address was that knowledge and enlightenment are the great peacemakers of the world, and that the *Sociedad patriótica de Lima* should employ all its mental force in placing Peruvians in possession of the secret on which depends their prosperity, expanding the horizon of their ideas, making popular the principles of a sane philosophy, developing a love of order, and fortifying their adherence to liberty and law. He summoned his compatriots to make war on the principles of the Spaniards, on their absurd ideas, their servile maxims, in a word on ignorance, which he declared to be the synonym of slavery and anarchy. In this the orator gave voice to one of the especially prominent ideas of revolutionary philosophy: that Spain tolerated popular ignorance, and ignorance kept the colonists victims of tyranny; and that enlightenment would make them free and ensure their prosperity.

After Monteagudo's address San Martín offered his protection to the society both as the chief magistrate of the state and as a private person. With this ceremony the society was officially established (61).

The first general meeting after the completion of the organization, February 22nd, 1822, agreed that the society should issue two periodicals: the first, a weekly, designed to contain short articles that might be generally instructive; the second, a quarterly, in which should appear more elaborate and extensive papers and addresses. The political purpose of the society is indicated by the subjects announced either for prize essays or for discussions by the members: 1. "What is the form of government best adapted to the Peruvian state, considering its extent, population, customs, and the grade of its civilization?" 2. "The causes that have retarded the revolution in Perú." 3. "The necessity of maintaining public order to terminate war and perpetuate peace." When it was proposed in the session of March 1st to debate the first question Señor Xavier de Luna Pizarro was of the opinion it should not be discussed except by the congress. Nevertheless after an exchange of opinions on this proposition, Monteagudo, the president, entered and ruled that all members might speak freely and that no one would be compromised by maintaining his opinion even though it might be in favour of the Spanish constitution (62).

Under this assurance the members entered upon a discussion of the question presented. Dr. José Ignacio Moreno spoke at length and argued with zeal against the acceptance of a democratic government for Perú. He emphasized the fact that Perú had never known any other than a monarchical government; that the inhabitants during several centuries had accustomed themselves to obedience to kings and to the turns and progress of affairs peculiar to a monarchical administration; that they were habituated to a prepossession in favour of rank, of distinctions of honour, and of inequality of possessions, all of which were matters incompatible with rigorous democracy; moreover, that this habit of mind was common to all classes in the state; and that among the Indians it was the most radical, since it was descended from the most remote antiquity of an empire always held in reverent affection (63). And the speaker reached the conclusion that the democratic form of government was not adapted to Perú whether considered with reference to the quality of Peruvian civilization, the population, and the customs, or the great extent of the territory (64).

The discussion of this question was continued in the session of March 8th. Dr. Manuel Pérez de Tudela opposed the thesis supported by Moreno, and maintained that the essence of society involved the liberty of the individual members, their security and equality before the law, their union in opposition to the enemy, fidelity to agreements, and hostility to whatever tends to disturb the public order. He asserted, moreover, that in the attainment of these ends some nations confided the administration to a single person; in others a part ruled and the rest obeyed; while a few were divided into different groups, or bodies, which aimed to maintain themselves in equilibrium, and in this manner were formed the three powers of the state. Pointing out what he conceived to be the shortcomings of monarchy and aristocracy, Tudela argued that it was of the nature of free government so to regulate the exercise of the sovereign power that the citizen might be exempt from all arbitrary authority, and that force might be employed to repress license. At the same time he made an extensive application of his doctrine to Perú as a free state. In concluding he said: "We all aspire to liberty, and we shall not be able to attain it, except by union among ourselves against the common despot and his satellites" (65). After the reading of Tudela's paper Marino José de Arce, an ecclesiastic, as was Moreno, took up the discussion, approved of Tudela's ideas as very just, and concluded " that the arguments of Señor Moreno, in spite of their eloquence, did not convince him, perhaps because of their identity with those which he had heard many times, presented to sustain the sceptre of Fernando VII " (66).

Dr. Fernando López Aldana, following, expressed the thought that before pronouncing in favour of monarchy it would be well to consider who was to be the monarch; whether a descendant of the Incas, a European prince, or some person who had played a prominent rôle in the revolution: the first would be attended with serious evils; the second would be degrading to America; and, in the third case, San Martín would be the logical candidate, and he was not available, since he was determined, after he had secured the liberty of the country, to end his days in retirement. The presentation of these practical suggestions aroused vigorous opposition; Antonio Alvarez del Villar declared that they were assembled only for the purpose of discussing questions theoretically. A lively discussion followed until the session was suspended. The last phase of the meeting was characterized by a clash of opinions that deprived it of its deliberative quality (67).

A week later the society returned to the question already considered. The members taking part in the discussion had apparently been influenced by the previous demand that the treatment of the subject should be purely theoretical; they were consequently led into various byways of philosophical obscurity. The monarchists had, however, in support of their views the disappearance of the revolutionary republics in Europe and the establishment of liberal monarchies in their place; and appeal was naturally made to the classical example of England. And in a subsequent meeting (March 15th), Dr. José Cavero y Salazar emphasized the fact that constitutional monarchy embraced many features desired by republicans: that the executive power residing in a king would withhold the state from anarchy; that the popular will would be respected, since the legislative power would be vested in an assembly or assemblies elected by the people.

Many serious persons entertained the thought that because of political inexperience the new states as republics were in danger of falling into anarchy, and this was for them a sufficient reason for advocating a monarchical form of government for Perú. This danger powerfully impressed Señor Aguirre, who affirmed that all peoples were at first governed by monarchs, and that republics appeared in the world after the habits and customs had become corrupted. Evidently terrified by what happened to France in becoming a republic through revolution, he drew a highly coloured picture of what might be expected in a republic (68).

If Perú had suffered under monarchy, it was not because of the form of government, but as a consequence of the covetousness manifested by the superior authority, and sometimes by the order of a stupid cabinet misled by sinister reports. By divesting the king of absolute power the people of a kingdom may be both free and happy.

The discussion of March 22nd
turned on the second of the general
topics that had been previously announced, that concerning the causes
which had retarded the revolution in
Perú. Two important causes were
pointed out, namely, the means taken
beforehand by Viceroy Abascal to make
impossible an uprising either in the
capital or in the provinces, and the
lack of a revolutionary leader. The
most elaborate contribution to the discussion of this subject was the paper by
José Morales, read at the meeting of
April 12th. Touching the attitude of
the merchants and nobles, to refer to a
single point of the discourse, he called
attention to the fact that there was
scarcely a creole merchant in Lima; the
majority were Europeans; and that in
order to retain their ancient monopoly,
they maintained a close and indissoluble
league with the government. The
nobles had their wealth in landed estates
or other real property, the principal

value of which consisted in the larger or smaller numbers of slaves who cultivated these lands; they were, therefore, naturally anxious to preserve the government which had created and approved of the system under which they had acquired their wealth (69).

Sessions of the society, according to the minutes deposited by the secretary in the National Library at Lima, continued to be held until July 12th, 1822. The discussions in some of the later meetings dealt with subjects in medicine and other departments of science, but the majority of the members and the majority of thoughtful persons in the country remained interested chiefly in political questions; and the debate was carried on in the congress and in periodical publications, in which Sánchez Carrión was especially prominent. In the *Abeja republicana* and in the *Correo mercantil*, he combated the ideas of Monteagudo. Ricardo Palma wrote

in 1877, " these two adversaries were
worthy of one another. Both were in
the fullness of life, profound thinkers,
eloquent, writing with equal vigour and
elegance in defense of their doctrines.
The republicans surrounded Sánchez
Carrión, and tacitly recognized him as
their leader, and obliged him to organ-
ize the resistance . . . He saved the
republic, and made monarchy in Perú
impossible " (70). This was, however,
accomplished only after contending
with increased monarchical forces;
for while the withdrawal of San
Martín from Perú removed one advocate of monarchy, it made way for the
appearance of another, in the person of
Bolívar, with even more extreme views
and a greater prestige. He came, moreover, accompanied by Monteagudo, who
as a man of thought supplemented the
man of action.

After the victory by the patriots at
Ayacucho under Sucre, December 9th,
1824, Bolívar, as dictator, appeared to

be in a position to attain the object of his ambition, and establish a monarchical government in Perú. The congress accepted his opinions and assumed an attitude of subserviency, and the bulk of the people joined in the triumph of the Liberator. But Monteagudo was murdered, and in the reaction from this popular enthusiasm, the prospects of an acknowledged monarchy in Perú disappeared.

The proceedings of the *Sociedad patriótica de Lima* may be taken as an illustrative instance of the numerous discussions that were held in different parts of Spanish South America, but they were not all conducted with equal formality. All appear to have been carried on with a patriotic purpose, and with a sincere desire for the welfare of the country. A benevolent ambition found expression not only in their search for a proper form of government, but also in many of the humane policies which they advocated; in the emancipation of the slaves, in establishing public libraries, in permitting books to be imported freely, and in giving prominence to means for providing public instruction.

IX

As the revolution continued and the final triumph seemed assured, many of the leaders turned their attention to topics relating to governmental organization. On these subjects there was a wide diversity of views, and in many cases the ideas of individual persons underwent extensive changes during the course of the conflict.

One of the reactions from the centralization of power that prevailed during the colonial period was a strong drift towards local autonomy. This movement was upheld by the fact that the *cabildo, ayuntamiento,* or municipal council, was practically the only institution that had root in the soil, the only important institution that survived the destruction of the viceregal régime; it was the sole remaining centre of legitimate power, and as such the revolutionists made use of it for their base of operations.

In this respect the Spanish colonies stood in strong contrast with the British colonies of North America. When the British colonies became independent, they carried into their new status governments with all departments in operation; and continued these governments which had come into existence under the force of custom and legislation. The Spanish colonists, on the other hand, had before them an unoccupied field in which their constructive imaginations might range freely. Under these conditions the wonder is not that there was a considerable variety of plans; but that there were brought to light so few political vagaries.

In Argentina the congress of Tucumán, organized on the 25th of March, 1816, had before it two principal projects, that of independence, and that concerning the form of the government that should be created for the country. Regarding the first there was essential unanimity; regarding the second there was a conspicuous diversity of opinions. There were advocates of monarchy who were doubtless monarchists by sincere conviction. Prominent among these were Dr. Acevedo, San Martín, and Belgrano. There were others, whose ideal government was a republic, but who were disposed to turn to monarchy as a means of stemming the rising tide of anarchy that threatened to destroy the social order in the name of democracy.

In view of a certain recognized individuality of the provinces in New Granada as in the viceroyalty of Río de la Plata, the proclamation of independence left the several provinces in doubt as to what this independence signified with respect to their position. This uncertainty gave ground for a controversy between the capital and the provinces.

In some cases the provinces put forth extravagant demands, which could not be recognized by the capital; and a voluminous debate sometimes attended this divergence of opinions. This was a feature of the revolution in New Granada. In the Argentine Republic it produced a civil war. Everywhere in the writings on the projected governments the controversy took the form of a discussion of the comparative merits of federal and centralized government.

In the beginning of his career in Buenos Aires, Monteagudo was the champion of a more or less vague conception of democracy, but in the course of time his contemplation of the indifference, the inexperience, and the ignorance of the inhabitants led him to seek some person or centralized institution that might furnish effective direction to the democratic multitude. This he found in a dictatorship, the creation of which he urged with special force (71).

This institution appeared to him consistent with the view that "sovereignty resides only in the people" and "that the general will is the only source from which emanate the sanctions of authority and power" (72). A dictatorship did not necessarily involve a violation of liberty; for a government of this form might be just, and just institutions were essential to liberty. In making political liberty synonymous with national independence and in calling the liberty of the individual citizen civil liberty he assumed to be following a British view (73). The dictator, as conceived by Monteagudo, was an all-powerful administrator with a definite term of authority entirely compatible with the imprescriptible right which every man possesses of discussing, speaking, and acting, in so far as he does not prejudice the rights and liberty of any other person, or contravene the justice he owes to himself; but the equality meant was not a social equality (74) but equality before the law. "Men are indeed equal, but this equality does not abrogate the superiority which some persons may have with respect to others by the very force of social conventions" (75). He decried "confounding equality with its abuses; all the rights of man have a moral limitation, the greatest transgression of which is a step towards injustice and disorder" (76).

Although in these early years Monteagudo was moved by a fiery zeal for liberty and the independence of his country he nevertheless recognized that "a people which passes suddenly from servitude to liberty is in imminent danger of precipitating itself into anarchy and falling back into slavery" (77).

In his practical activity Monteagudo was a whirlwind of passion and energy, but the movement of his mind in his philosophical contemplation was coolly reasonable, and affirmed the importance of moderation. "No people," he wrote, "was ever free without being moderate," and the formula, "No right without its corresponding duty," (78) often repeated and emphasized, appears in his early writings.

Monteagudo's impatience of the stagnant colonial life carried him almost immediately to extremes. This spirit found expression not only in the name of his periodical, *El Mártir ó Libre*, but also in its closing words when it was discontinued for lack of public support, "La independencia ó el sepulcro, la libertad ó la muerte." Monteagudo's impatience of conflicting voices in government, and of the delays and inefficiency of assemblies made him the partisan and advocate of a personal dictatorship. In an article published in *El Mártir ó Libre*, April 6th, 1812, he set forth definitely this view:

"I believe that one of the means best adapted to our condition would be to concentrate authority in a single citizen

enjoying public confidence, to make him
responsible for the conduct of the army
and for the execution of all measures
concerning public affairs; in a word, to
place no other limit to his powers than
the independence of the country, leaving to his will the appointment of the
persons most perfectly qualified for
office in each of the branches of the
administration; and to prescribe the
period when, in accordance with the re-
quirements of the public, this magistracy
should expire, and such other rules as
ought to be adopted."

Whether advocating democracy or
monarchy, Monteagudo never lacked
zeal in promulgating his ideas. At first
his propaganda was supported only by
his proper personality and the reasonableness of his views. Later, however,
during his association with San Martín,
his advocacy was strengthened by that
general's great prestige. There was no
loss of force through clashing doctrines.
The Protector and his minister enjoyed

a noteworthy intellectual sympathy; yet
San Martín came late to the expression
of his political opinions. While creating his army in Mendoza, carrying on
the war in Chile, and leading his forces
to Perú, San Martín's mind was completely absorbed by the endless details
of his military affairs. His correspondence bears almost exclusively on this
point. Until he arrived in Lima he
appears to have given little attention to
political questions. His letters to
O'Higgins concerned only the army
and the means necessary to make possible the expedition to Perú (79).

When he finally turned to the practical business of organizing a state, he
proceeded on the basis of his views respecting the proper application of
liberty. In his opinion, "the work of
difficulty, and that which must be
courageously, firmly and circumspectly
undertaken, is to correct the vague ideas
which the former government has left
impressed on the minds of the present

generation. It is not to be supposed, however, that this difficulty consists so much in the want of acquaintance with the adequate means by which the end is to be accomplished, as in the dangerous precipitancy with which new governments reform the abuses they find established. Liberty, the most ardent of our wishes, must be restored with caution, in order that the sacrifices which are made for the purpose of gaining it be not rendered useless. Every civilized people is in a state to be free; but the degree of freedom, which a country can enjoy, ought to bear an exact ratio to the measure of its civilization: if the first exceeds the last, no power can save them from anarchy; and if the reverse happen, namely that the degree of civilization goes beyond the amount of freedom which the people possess, oppression is the consequence. If all Europe were suddenly to be put in possession of the liberty of England, the greater part of it would present a complete chaos; and if, instead of their present constitution, the English were to be subjected to the charter of Louis XVIII, they would consider themselves enslaved. It is right that the governments of South America be free; but it is necessary they should be so in the proportion stated; the greatest triumph of our enemies would be to see us depart from that measure " (80).

Monteagudo continued to preach monarchical doctrines, but those persons who supported the republican program, aroused by his astonishing activity, formed a union under the leadership of Sánchez Carrión to promote interest in democracy and adhesion to a democratic party. The opposition to Monteagudo was increased by that minister's arrogance, his personal extravagance, and his luxurious style of living. These characteristics became especially manifest after San Martín's departure from Lima, to confer with

Bolívar at Guayaquil. The conflict between these two parties, the champions of monarchy on the one hand, and the advocates of a republican government on the other, led to the removal of Monteagudo from the ministry, and his banishment from Perú.

Concerning his service in the cause of liberty Monteagudo has left the following statement: " From the 25th of May, 1809, my thoughts and my whole being were consecrated to the revolution: I found myself accidentally in the city of La Plata (Chuquisaca) when that community, heroic and vehement in all its sentiments, gave the first example of rebellion; then it had no other name, for it is the good outcome which changes the designation. I took an active part in that affair with the honoured General Avenales, and other eminent patriots, who have become victims of the Spaniards. Since that day I have lived disinterestedly (*gratuitamente*); once condemned to death and at other times near it, I did not expect to survive such danger. My great suffering and the incorrect ideas which I then had of the nature of government, made me embrace with fanaticism the democratic system. Rousseau's *Social contract* and other writings of that kind, as it appeared to me, were favourable to despotism. Of the periodicals which I published during the revolution, I wrote none with more ardour than *El Mártir ó Libre,* which appeared in Buenos Aires. To be a patriot without being mad for democracy was for me a contradiction, and this was my view. In order to expiate my early (*premenos*) errors, I published in Chile in 1819, *El Censor de la revolución.* I had already recovered from this kind of mental fever, from which almost all of us have suffered; and he is unfortunate who in the course of time is not cured of it.

" When the liberating army arrived in Perú, my ideas were stamped with

the seal of twelve years of revolution.
The horrors of civil war, the backward-
ness of the cause of independence, the
ruin of a thousand families sacrificed
for absurd principles, finally, all the
vicissitudes of which I had been either
a spectator or the victim, naturally
made me think that it was necessary to
set aside the causes of such dreadful
effects.

"Entertaining these sentiments, I
could not be unfaithful to them when
circumstances gave me an active part in
the direction of affairs. On taking
upon myself the enormous task which I
have finished, I wrote in the *tabla* of
my duties the principles which my conscience dictated to me. I have followed
them strictly, and I hold to them firmly,
for I would rather be a thousand times
a victim of the revolution than unmind-
ful of them " (81).

Monteagudo's turning away from
democracy toward aristocracy and monarchy had a certain support in his view

that the danger to be feared was not a drift towards despotism, but the growing disposition to refuse obedience to the government (82). Throughout his career Monteagudo's views on political affairs were not mere theoretical opinions but served as his chief guide in practical conduct. While others, also zealous in the patriots' cause, adapted themselves to the changing ideas and changing policies of the time, he clashed with them as the champion of his individual opinions and plans. For his stubbornness he was thrice sent into exile, but he was not thus to be set aside. He was both feared as an opponent and found to be an essential factor in the movement for independence.

Whatever may have been San Martín's original views respecting a form of government for the emancipated colonies, when he became Protector of Perú he was in sympathy with Monteagudo, and together with him, Pueyrredón, and O'Higgins, laboured to establish monarchy in America. For this purpose O'Higgins instructed the Chilean minister Irisarri, Pueyrredón commissioned Rivadavia, and San Martín and Monteagudo ordered García del Río and Parroissien to go to Europe to seek princes who might be established as kings in Chile, Argentina, and such other divisions as might be set apart as separate states. Prominent supporters of this project in Perú — San Martín, Monteagudo, Unánue, Moreno, Echague, and Torre-Tagle — set themselves to prepare the public to accord a favourable reception to the proposed rulers.

San Martín landed in Perú on the 28th of July, 1821, and on the 3rd of August following he issued at Lima a proclamation announcing the organization of the government of Perú. After setting forth his aims respecting the welfare of the country he pledged his word in the most solemn manner, to the people of Perú, " that from the very moment the foreign enemy shall be expelled from this territory, I will resign the command to make room for the government they may wish to constitute " (83). In the same document he further announced:

" It being evidently conformable to the interests of the country, that a vigorous government should be established, such an one as may be enabled effectually to shield it from the evils to which war, license, and anarchy might give rise, I have therefore been induced to decree that the supreme political and military command of the free department of Perú are from the date hereof, united to my person under the title Protector."

The *Provisional Statute*, embodying apparently the ideas of the four signers of the document, provided that the Catholic, Apostolic, and Roman religion should be the religion of the state, and that no one could be a public functionary unless he professed that religion.

The supreme executive power in this state should reside in the Protector of Perú, who should be the commander-in-chief of the sea and land forces. He might levy taxes, establish duties, and negotiate loans. He should make rules for the organization of the naval and land forces; should regulate interior and exterior commerce; should introduce such reforms as he might think necessary, should establish the provisional coinage, but might not alter the weight or standard of the coin current in Perú. He should appoint envoys and consuls to foreign courts, and promote the acknowledgement of Peruvian independence by such diplomatic and commercial agreements as might be for the interest of the country.

The ministers of state, at first three, were the chiefs of their respective departments. There was also provided a council of state composed of twelve members including the three ministers and other high civil, military, and ecclesiastical officials.

In place of the ancient audiencia there was established, by the *Provisional Statute*, a supreme court known as the High Chamber of Justice, having judicial attributes formerly possessed by the ancient court (84). In the *Provisional Statute*, San Martín says, " I shall, however, abstain from interfering, in any way, with the solemn exercise of the judicial functions, because their independence is the only and true safeguard of the people's liberties; and of little avail is it to make an ostentatious boast of maxims exquisitely philanthropic, when he who makes the law, is also he who applies it " (85). Under the *Provisional Statute* the forms of local government remained, with only such changes as were necessary to adapt them to the new general organization (86).

After the creation of governments for the several states, Argentina, Chile and the others, the logical step was to a consideration of the relation which these states should hold to one another. The question of a union of states was naturally suggested by the fact that in many cases cities as heads of districts, particularly in New Granada, had separately declared for independence, and had later been drawn together under a national government. San Martín appears to have been the first to be profoundly influenced in his actions by the thought of the mutual dependence of the several states, that the liberty of one depended on the liberty of all. This was the underlying motive of his plan to take an army into Chile, and later to proceed to the liberation of Perú.

The earliest conception of the *Unión americana* appears to have been set forth by him in his proclamation of November 13th, 1818, *A los limeños y habitantes de todo el Perú*, in which he said, " The union of the three independent states (Buenos Aires, Chile, and Perú) will result in inspiring in Spain the sentiment of its impotence, and in the other powers that of esteem and respect. These first steps of your political existence having been secured, a central congress, composed of representatives of these three states, will give to their respective organizations a new stability, and the constitution of each as well as its alliance and perpetual federation will be established in the midst of enlightenment, concord, and universal hope " (87). On this point, as on almost all points concerning political organization, the division of opinions continued long after the close of the first period of constitution-making.

The discussion of an inter-state union was now and then varied by a consideration of federal organization of the individual states as opposed to a project for a centralized government. The champions of federation urged that the successful progress of the United States furnished a conclusive argument in favour of adopting the federal form of government for the people.

This was a view that became widely accepted in the several states, and many persons presented drafts of constitutions, embodying the essential features of the constitution of the United States.

In the political discussion at Bogotá in 1811 Camilo Torres supported the plan for a federation, while Antonio Nariño advocated a centralized government for the whole country (88).

Monteagudo was convinced that the republic of the United States, in the brief period of its existence, had not shown that the government was anything more than an experiment, saying, " We are not able to be as free as those who were born in that classic land, England, which has presented the model of constitutional government, nor as free as the democrats of North America, who, educated in the school of liberty, dare to make the experiment of a form of government, whose excellence has not been satisfactorily proved by its continuance for forty-four years."

The foregoing pages of this chapter present the noteworthy fact that the most conspicuous leaders of the revolution favoured some form of monarchy for the new states instead of any form of a republic. Approval of monarchical rule might have been expected of persons who had created armies and led them successfully to battle, or of persons engaged in the administration of military affairs. The spread of knowledge and the awakening of popular interest in politics was followed by a rising tide of republican sentiment, which ultimately overwhelmed the opinions of the leaders. A phase of the conflict of ideas is seen in the debates, or discussions, conducted by the patriotic societies.   Between 1820 and the end of the revolutionary period, Lima was the principal centre for the exchange of political opinions.

X

A clear conception of Simón Bolívar's contribution to the intellectual background of the revolution can be obtained only by taking account of his profound emotions and of his vivid and changing visions. An illustration of his emotional nature is furnished by the account of his experience in the great romance of his life. Writing from Madrid September 10th, 1800, at the age of seventeen, he described with enthusiasm the love he had conceived for Señorita Teresa de Toro, a Venezuelan and one of his distant relatives. Near the end of the next year he married her at Madrid, and in June 1803, ten months after their arrival at Caracas, she died. Bolívar never married again, and for many months after this event he suffered serious

mental depression, to such an extent
that life did not seem to him worth
living. In 1804, he had, however,
sufficiently recovered to enter into an
intimate friendship with Fanny Servieu
du Villars. Madame du Villars was the
daughter of the Baroness de Torbriano,
who was Bolívar's cousin, and at that
time was twenty-eight years old, while
Bolívar was twenty-one. In a letter to
her, written in 1804, the future Liberator recounted some phases of his experience subsequent to the death of his
young wife. Madame du Villars's
prominence in Parisian society is seen in
the fact that her salon was frequented
by such conspicuous persons as Madame
Récamier, Madame de Staël, and
Prince Eugene; by distinguished statesmen, generals, and savants. In the
letter referred to, Bolívar called
Madame du Villars Teresa, perhaps
making her the object of the affection he had entertained for Teresa de
Toro.

"You should remember," he wrote,
"how sad I was when I abandoned
you to join Señor Rodríguez in Vienna.
I expected much from the society of
my friend, the companion of my child-
hood, the confidant in all my joys and
sorrows, the mentor whose counsels and
consolation have always had so much
weight with me. Alas, in these circumstances his friendship was sterile.
Señor Rodríguez only loves the sciences.
My tears do not affect him, although
he sincerely likes me, but he does not
understand them. I found him occupied in a chemical and physical
laboratory belonging to a German, and
in which experiments in these sciences
were publicly made by Señor Rodríguez. I saw him scarcely an hour a
day. When we met he said to me in
a hurry, 'My friend, amuse yourself,
find persons of your own age, go to the
theatre, in a word, you must distract
yourself, and this is the only means by
which you may cure yourself.' I under-

stand now there is something lacking in this man, the wisest, the most virtuous and, doubtless, the most extraordinary man one may meet. I fell very soon into consumption, and the doctor declared that I was going to die; that was what I wished. One night I was very ill, Rodríguez and my physician awakened me; both spoke in German. I did not understand a single word of what they said, but in their tone and in the expression of their faces, I saw that their conversation was very animated. The physician, after he had examined me thoroughly, went away. I was in complete possession of my senses, and although very weak I was still able to carry on a conversation. Rodríguez came and sat down by me, spoke to me with the kindness and affection which he has always manifested towards me in the most serious circumstances of my life. He mildly reproved me, and assured me that this giving-up and wishing to die in the middle of life

was a crazy idea. He made me understand that there are other things than
love in the life of men; that I might
be very happy devoting myself to
science, and giving myself up to ambition. You know with what persuasive
enchantment this man speaks; although
he may utter the most absurd sophisms,
one believes that he is right. He per-
suades me, as he does every one he
wishes to. Seeing me a little better, he
left me, but the next day he repeated
the same exhortations. The following
night, my imagination excited by all
that I might do, whether for science or
for the liberty of the people, I said to
him, 'Yes, without doubt, I feel that
I could throw myself into the brilliant
careers which you present to me, but it
would be necessary that I should be
rich. Without means for carrying out
plans, nothing is accomplished, and, far
from being rich, I am poor, and I am ill
and broken in spirit. Ah, Rodríguez,
I prefer to die.' I gave him my hand,

in order to beg him to let me die in
peace. Then I saw a sudden change
in Rodríguez's expression; he remained
a moment in doubt, like a man who
vacillates as to the part he ought to
take. Then in an instant he raised his
eyes and hands towards heaven, ex-
claiming in an inspired voice, 'He is
saved.' He came to me, took my hands,
opened them in his, which were trem-
bling and were bathed in perspiration,
and then said to me in a very af-
fectionate tone, 'My friend, if you
were rich, would you consent to live?
Speak. Answer me.' I replied 'Yes.'
'Ah,' he exclaimed, 'then we are
saved. Gold, after all, may be good
for something. Very well, then,
Simón Bolívar, you are rich. You have
actually four millions.' I shall not
picture to you, dear Teresa, the impres-
sion which these words made upon me,
'You have actually four millions.' As
extensive and rich as our Spanish language is, it is, as are all others, im-

potent to explain such emotions. Men experience them only a few times; their words correspond to the ordinary sentiments of the world; those which I felt were superhuman. I am astonished that my organization was able to stand them.

" I pause; the memory which I have just evoked overwhelms me.

" Oh, how far are riches from giving the pleasures which they make us expect! "

In later years Bolívar's driving emotions and his glowing imagination, revealing victory where others saw only defeat, made him the unrivaled hero of the revolution. He won his military successes not through special knowledge of the accepted rules of war, but by an inspiration, a vision, a dashing leadership that defied all rules. His enthusiasm for the war as a means to liberty is seen in his letter to President Nariño, May 10th, 1813, expressing his appreciation of the troops sent to him by the government of Cundinamarca:

" What a beautiful spectacle is presented, Señor Presidente, on the stage of New Granada, which is going to see a struggle perhaps unique in history: to see, I say, men running freely and simultaneously from all the towns of New Granada for the reëstablishment of liberty, and of the independence of the extinguished republic of Venezuela, without other stimulus than humanity; with no other ambition than that of the glory of breaking the chains which are dragging along their compatriots; and with no other hope than the reward which virtue gives to the heroes who fight for reason and justice " (89). In politics his views were flashes of imagination rather than the studied conclusions of deliberate thought. He never pledged himself to consistency but spoke as the visions flitted across his mind.

In Venezuela, as in New Granada and in Chile, the first successes of the patriots were followed by defeat and a temporary domination of the royalists. During this period Bolívar had occasion to reflect on the difficulties the patriots had to face, and to formulate principles to be applied in their work of political construction. During a part of this period Bolívar was in Jamaica. In a letter written at Kingston September 6th, 1815, he gave expression to certain doctrines that then formed the basis of his social philosophy. These doctrines are for the greater part stated with reference to the concrete facts of Spanish America. He agreed with M. de Pradt that the region in question should be divided into a number of states, but disagreed with him in affirming that these states should be governed as republics, not as monarchies. The reason advanced in support of the plan for creating small republics, instead of one large state, was the thought that small republics are permanent, while large republics change, become " decadent, convert their free forms into tyrannical forms, relax the principles designed to preserve them, and run ultimately into despotism. Almost all of the small republics have lasted long; of the large republics, only Rome maintained itself for several centuries, and this was because the capital only and not the rest of the dominion was a republic; the provinces were governed by different laws and institutions. Quite the reverse of this is the policy of a king, whose constant inclination is to increase his possessions, riches, and prerogatives; and this with reason, for his authority increases with these acquisitions, as well with respect to foreign affairs as with regard to his own subjects, who fear his power as his dominion becomes more formidable, which is preserved by means of war and conquests " (90).

In contemplating governments for the proposed Spanish-American states, Bolívar rejected the proposition to apply the federal system, " as being too perfect; and requiring virtues and political talents much superior to those possessed by the Spanish Americans in the early years of the nineteenth century." He also rejected the mixed monarchical government, embracing aristocracy and democracy, " which had brought such freedom and splendour to England " (91). Such a government, he held, would depart from a just balance by the preponderance of one party or another. "If the preponderant party is military or aristocratic, it may demand a monarchy, which, in the beginning, will be limited and constitutional, and which afterwards will inevitably decline, and become absolute; " for " there is nothing in the political order more difficult than the preservation of a mixed monarchy." " Only a people as patriotic as the English is capable of restraining the authority of a king, and of maintaining the spirit of liberty under a sceptre and a crown " (92).

During the progress of the revolution, Bolívar, unlike San Martín, took an active part in political organization. He believed that the governments to be formed for the new states should be republican; but in these republics the executive should have extensive prerogatives, and the prerogatives should be held by a person who should perform his functions with prudence and justice; and it might, moreover, be expected that there would be a tendency for him to continue in authority for life. In spite of the extensive powers accredited to the executive, the government contemplated was a representative republic. In Bolívar's view, however, there were real limits to the application of the representative principle. Inasmuch as the people of the emancipated colonies "had not acquired the talents and political virtues which distinguish our brethren of the North, systems entirely popular are far from being favourable for us" (93).

Bolívar was doubtless moved to emphasize the power and tenure of the republican executive by the desire to find or create a stable element in a government which he regarded as lacking in harmony and stability; for in his view " almost all of the republics that have inspired in the human race the greatest veneration have carried within themselves the seeds of mortal discord, and this has provoked the saying that disunion is often the thermometer indicating the degree of liberty; and that the success of a government liberally constituted is, in general, in direct ratio to the fervour of parties and the clash of political opinions. It is true that the burden of liberty is light, but still it is difficult to maintain it in equilibrium, even in the nations most cultivated and civilized " (94).

The notion of liberty entertained by Bolívar is sufficiently announced in a letter written by him at San Cristóbal,

May 26th, 1820, and addressed to
William White. In this letter he affirms that " there is no legitimate liberty
except where it is employed to honour
humanity and improve its lot, or
fortune " (95).

Bolívar also had visions of an international union. He conceived of all
parts of the emancipated dominions
bound together and forming a single
nation. Seeing that all had a common
origin, common customs, and a common religion, they ought, consequently,
" to have a single government that
would unite the different states that
might be formed; but this is not possible, because distant climates, diverse
situations, opposing interests and unlike
characters divide America. How fine it
would be if the Isthmus of Panamá
might be for us what the Isthmus of
Corinth was for the Greeks! Would
that some day we may have the good
fortune to install there an august congress of the representatives of the

republics, kingdoms, and empires, to confer and discuss concerning the important interests of peace and war with the nations of the other three parts of the world " (96).

Bolívar's plan for a comprehensive international union was more than a passing thought, as is indicated by his work in behalf of the congress of Panamá. Like other visionaries before and after him it seemed to him only a short step from centuries of war to a millennium of peace. He had battered down the long-established walls of Spanish power and tradition, and by the brutal force of arms had ushered in a new and better time, yet, with the noise of the battle for liberty ringing in his ears he dreamed that thenceforth the good things of life, freedom from tyranny, the security of home and family from the lawless within and the invaders from without, were to be achieved and maintained without the use of force. It was the Utopian

vision of a final war. Others have had
the same vision in later days, even while
contributing to conditions prolific of
war.

Bolívar's conduct of the military and
political affairs of the rebellion in the
north displays clear practical sense,
and his writings indicate that his de-
cisions were not without an underlying ground of general principles.
These principles he did not embody
in a formal political treatise, but
they appear spontaneously here and
there in his letters. They make manifest the error of regarding him as
merely a radical with capacity only for
agitation and fighting. His career revealed, indeed, a certain radicalism, in
the creation of a new method of
making war. In opposition to this his
antagonists followed the rigid rules acquired in the European schools of
tactics; and in actual conflict they were
at a distinct disadvantage and were
frequently overwhelmed, although

commanding superior numbers of experienced soldiers.

But in politics he was conservative, as were nearly all of the prominent leaders in the great enterprise. He recognized the necessity of adapting the form of government to the state of the society where it is established, and in this manner he raised a question which the modern radical is seldom disposed to consider. Even the government of the United States, conservative as it was in the early decades of the nineteenth century, appeared to him too radical for the new states of South America.

We speak of the movement of society as if it were a great unwieldy animal, writhing and twisting, trying to propel its immense mass by a certain centralized internal force. This is an extreme view which fails to embrace the fact that the force which moves society, when traced to its origin, is the will of an independent, self-conscious person, or a small group of such persons.

The results of Bolívar's attempts to apply his ideas in governmental organization are seen in his drafts of constitutional laws, one presented to the congress of Angostura, the other designed as the basis of a government for Bolivia.

The congress of Angostura met on the 15th of February, 1819. At this meeting Bolívar presented the draft of a constitution, made by himself in collaboration with Francisco Antonio Zea, and in his discourse introducing it set forth certain principles which appeared to him necessary to the successful conduct of popular government. There should be repeated elections, " since nothing is so dangerous as letting power remain for a long time in the hands of the same person. The people become accustomed to obeying him, and he becomes accustomed to commanding them; whence usurpation and tyranny arise. A just zeal is the guarantee of liberty, and our citizens ought to fear, with bold justice, that the same magistrate who has governed them for a long time, may govern them perpetually " (97).

While Bolívar recognized that it was necessary to maintain equality and liberty in a republic, he nevertheless held that the senate should not be elective but hereditary, " for there must exist in every government a neutral body that may assume the part of the offended and disarm the offender. This neutral body, in order that it may be such, ought not to owe its origin either to appointment by the government or to election by the people, so that it may enjoy complete independence, and neither fear nor hope anything from these two sources of authority. An hereditary senate will be the fundamental basis of the legislative power, and consequently will be the basis of the whole government. It will equally serve as a counterpoise to the government and to the people; it will be an intermediate power that will nullify the shots which these eternal rivals discharge at one another. In all the controversies, the calmness of a third authority may serve as an agency for reconciliation."

The disposition of the several provinces in Venezuela and Colombia to form constitutions and set up independent administrations confirmed Bolívar in the view that whatever might be the theoretical excellence of federal government, his countrymen were not prepared to adopt it practically. "Unity," he said with special emphasis, "should be our motto." "For however attractive may appear and be in effect this magnificent federal system, it has not been given us to enjoy it immediately on escaping from chains. Our moral constitution has not as yet the necessary consistency to receive benefit from a government completely representative and so sublime that it might be adapted to a republic of saints."

"One should not forget that the excellence of a government does not consist in its theory, in its form, nor in its mechanism but in being appropriate to the nature and the character of the nation for which it is instituted" (98).

While Bolívar was an ardent republican, he had nevertheless reasonable doubts as to the fitness of the South Americans for exercising all the rights and prerogatives presumed to belong to citizens of a democratic republic; they lacked the requisite character, habits, and enlightenment (99).

In spite of the fact that Bolívar was involved in the "war to the death", virtually a civil war, in which both Spaniards and a considerable part of the inhabitants fought as royalists, he held that it was good policy in civil wars to be generous, since the spirit of revenge increases with the continuance of the conflict (100).

The constitution of the Republic of Colombia, based on the draft presented

by Bolívar to the congress of Angostura, was finally adopted on the 6th of
October, 1821. It provided for an
essentially centralized government, in
opposition to the sentiment of a considerable party in favour of a large
measure of local independence and a
federal union. This document indicated a distinct development in the
spirit of the revolution; it shows, moreover, by its provisions, that the members
of the congress, who finally adopted it,
were influenced by the constitution of
the United States to omit or modify the
peculiar and more or less visionary
views of Bolívar. In the form which
it thus received at the congress of
Rosario de Cúcuta it served as a model
for certain constitutions adopted later in
some of the new states of South America, particularly in Colombia (101).

Now that the war was over, and his
military purposes had been achieved,
Bolívar's imagination turned its whole
constructive force upon government.

For a score of years the vision of a free
America had absorbed his attention and
controlled his activity. If the state
which he conceived had Utopian
features, it shows that Bolívar's later
opinions were consistent with those of
his earlier years. In his military undertakings, as well as in politics, his course
was largely determined by his creative
imagination. Where reason, whether
in war or peace, ordinarily restrained
others, Bolívar's vision prompted him
to act. He formed projects which the
unwinged critics and politicians thought
to be fantastic.

On the 6th of August, 1825, the
claims of the Provinces of Río de la
Plata for territory having been set
aside, the Assembly of Deputies of
Upper Perú declared Upper Perú an
independent republic, called the " Republic of Bolívar ", a title afterwards
changed to Bolivia. The republic
sought the protection of Bolívar, and
invited him to draft a constitution for

the state. At a meeting of its representatives, on the 25th of May, 1826, in a noteworthy discourse, he laid his project before the assembly, or constituent congress; which being adopted became the famous *Constitución boliviana.*

In Bolívar's address on this occasion, he indicated that his supreme purpose was to maintain liberty, equality, and internal peace. He recognized that liberty was threatened not only by tyranny, but also by anarchy. " Tyranny and anarchy " to quote his picturesque expression, " form an immense ocean of oppression, which surrounds a little island of liberty, perpetually battered by the violence of the waves and the hurricane, which advance upon it without ceasing, in an effort to submerge it " (102).

To the usual legislative, executive, and judicial branches of the government, Bolívar added a fourth branch, called the electoral. This was to consist of electors chosen by popular vote, every ten citizens choosing one elector, thus creating a national representation consisting of a tenth of the citizens. The electors of each province were to be organized and hold their meetings in the capital of the province, in January of each year. It devolved upon the electors to admit persons to citizenship and to suspend the rights of citizenship; to elect members of the legislature and certain provincial and local officials; to receive and verify the returns of the popular elections; to petition the legislative bodies, and to complain of grievances and instances of injustice. "In this manner," to quote Bolívar's introductory speech, "a new weight is placed in the balance against the executive, and government acquires more guarantees and new titles to superiority among democracies" (103).

It was provided that the legislature should be composed of three houses: the

Tribunes, the Senators, and the Censors, the tenure in each case being four years. Besides the ordinary duties and prerogatives of representative legislative bodies, the legislature as provided for, had the right to elect the first president and to confirm his successors; also to approve the vice president, appointed by the president. Each house, for the first twenty years, was to consist of thirty members, and it was expected by the author of the constitution that the participation of the three houses in legislation would prevent a deadlock. To the Tribunes who were elected for four years, was assigned the right to initiate laws on financial affairs, on peace, and on war. They were charged also with the inspection of certain branches of the executive administration. The Senate was expected to draft the civil and the criminal codes, to regulate ecclesiastical affairs and to supervise the courts. The idealism of Bolívar was especially expressed in the provisions relating to the Censors, who were elected for life. " The Censors," he affirmed, " exercise a political and moral power resembling that of the court of the Areopagus at Athens and the Censors at Rome." They were required to see that the constitution and public treaties were religiously observed, and to decide on the merits and demerits of the executive administration. To the Censors was referred the protection of morals, science, the arts, instruction, and the press. " The most terrible as well as the most august functions belong to the Censors. They may condemn to eternal ignominy usurpers of sovereign authority and notable criminals. They may grant public honours for the services and the virtues of illustrious citizens. The field of glory is confided to their hands; wherefore, the Censors must have untarnished characters and pure lives " (104).

The president should hold office for life; " the supreme authority ought to be perpetual, because in the systems without hierarchies it is more necessary than in others, that there should be a fixed point, around which the magistrates and the citizens should revolve " (105). The power exercised by the president of Bolivia, compared with that of the president of the United States, was limited in favour of the people. This limitation is seen partly in the fact that he cannot appoint either the executive officers or the judges. It was provided, however, that he should appoint the vice president, with the approval of the legislature, and the secretaries, without such approval; his power to remove them was unrestricted.

Finding in the principle of heredity the ground of monarchical stability, Bolívar sought to attain this end in the republic by giving the president the right to name his successor, and this was accomplished practically by recognizing the vice president as heir to the office of president (106).

The Bolivian constitution was designed not merely for Bolivia; its author wished to have it adopted by other states, and to unite the states thus organized in an imperial federation. It was adopted by Bolivia and especially by Perú, under the immediate influence of Bolívar and his Colombian troops, but the plan to have it adopted in Colombia failed.

The political ideas that here found expression were not the product of a sudden inspiration, but had been gradually taking shape during the years of his stormy experience. In his speech at the congress of Angostura, on the 15th of February, 1819, he urged that body " to adopt centralism and the reunion of all the states of Venezuela in a republic one and indivisible." At this time he had, moreover, the idea of a single president instead of a triumvirate or any other form of a collegiate executive. " The executive power in a republic," he affirmed, " must be strong, for all conspire against it. In a monarchy the power should rest in the legislature, for all conspire in favour of the monarch." "The bases of a republican government," he added, "must be the sovereignty of the people, the division of power, civil liberty, the proscription of slavery, and the abolition of monarchy and privileges." His arguments in favour of a hereditary upper house, or senate, with an elected representative lower house, point to the influence of the English constitution.

Certain prominent features of the Bolivian constitution were already in Bolívar's mind when he presented his draft of a fundamental law for Venezuela to the congress of Angostura. According to this project the president, although elected, should hold a position not greatly unlike that of the British king; but the members of the congress showed little sympathy with this view, and according to the constitution as adopted at Rosario de Cúcuta, in 1821,

the president was to be elected for a
period of four years, and might be
reëlected only once without an inter-
mission. The members of the senate
according to Bolívar's draft were to
be elected in the first instance, and
thereafter they were to be hereditary, but under the constitution as
finally adopted, they were to be elected
for eight years, and were not hereditary. The lower house, or the House
of Representatives, was to be similar to
that of the United States.

In addition to the president and the
two houses of congress Bolívar sought
to create an institution, the plan of
which he had had in mind for many
years. This was a body to supervise
public morals, and to seek to eliminate
all forms of corruption. In the Bolivian constitution, the provisions concerning the censors were to realize this
plan, by making them a third branch of
the legislature. In the congress of
Angostura and in that of Rosario de

Cúcuta, the members were more influenced by the institutions of the
United States than was Bolívar. The
seventh article of the constitution of
1821 seems to indicate that the creation of the city of Washington was
the model for their proposed capital.

"A new city, which shall bear the
name of the Liberator, Bolívar, shall
be the capital of the Republic of Colombia. Its plan and situation shall be
determined by the first general congress,
under the principle of adapting it to
the necessities of the three departments
and to the greatness to which this opulent country is destined by nature."

In numerous constitutional provisions, similar to provisions in the constitution of the United States, proposed
and adopted by the congress, the influence of the northern republic on that
body is clearly manifest, while Bolívar's
mind inclined rather towards British
institutions. They were apparently in
harmony in providing for trial by jury,

the freedom of the press, and guarantees of civil liberty.

The Bolivian constitution has been described as modeled on principles which appear to have been taken from the Republic of Venice. Arosemena wrote that it " excited much alarm by its provisions, which appeared opposed to liberty, and which consisted of a mixture of Roman, English, and American institutions, arranged with skill and, doubtless, in good faith " (107).

Many persons criticized it severely, perhaps more severely than would seem justified after a thorough inquiry into the condition of the country, and an examination of the powers granted to the various governmental agencies. The Bolivian congressional committee on constitutional affairs, to whom the project by Bolívar had been referred, reported enthusiastically in favour of it, declaring it the product of " experience and enlightenment, and the fruit of the most profound meditation." The report closed with the statement that " hitherto we have fought for independence; henceforth we ought to strive for the establishment and preservation of this constitution." The attitude in Perú and Colombia was very different from this; the Bolivian constitution was adopted in Perú, but practically under compulsion; it was rejected in Colombia (108).

XI

After fourteen years of conflict during which the tide of war had rolled
from victory to defeat and from defeat
to victory, the battle-worn revolutionists at last in 1824 saw the approaching
end of the struggle. Then the patriots,
whose minds had swung between hope
and fear, gave voice to their emotions
in songs of triumph. Many of these
songs, the spontaneous outbursts of joy,
were forgotten when the public mind
became absorbed in the gigantic task of
organizing free states where only
despotism had ruled. Later generations, however, have been glad to remember *La Victoria de Junín* and its
author José Joaquín de Olmedo. He
is remembered both for his constructive
work in the service of the revolution

and for his celebration of Bolívar's victories. Although his political plans were swept aside by Bolívar and his advancing troops, he did not hesitate to devote his spirited song to the glorification of the Liberator.

Olmedo was born in Guayaquil March 20th, 1780. His father was a member of a prominent family of Málaga, and landed in America in 1757, and for five years thereafter he was administrator of the royal revenues in Panamá. Later he was *corregidor* at Quito, and died at Guayaquil on the 27th of August, 1808. Two years after the death of his father, José Joaquín de Olmedo was elected to be a member of the Cortes at Cádiz, and on the 24th of August, 1812, he was appointed one of the secretaries of that body. It was the Cortes of Cádiz that formed the famous Constitution of 1812, and declared that it would not recognize the authority of Ferdinand the Seventh since he refused to take oath of fidelity to that instrument. One of the important legislative acts of the Cortes with respect to America was the abolition of the *mita*, or the law providing for forced labour by the Indians.

Returning from Spain to Guayaquil, Olmedo lived for four years withdrawn from all part in political affairs. This was the first period of his important literary activity; but in 1820 the progress of Bolívar in the north and of San Martín in the south provoked an uprising in Guayaquil, and Olmedo by the insistence of his fellow citizens became the head of the revolutionary movement. After the proclamation of independence, he was appointed chief of the provisional government. The ordinance establishing that government was written by Olmedo. It throws light on his political views at that time as well as on the views of his countrymen during those years when the province of Guayaquil was passing from the old régime to the new order of political affairs. The text of this ordinance follows:

PROVISIONAL ORDINANCE OF GOVERNMENT

Adopted by the Electoral Convention of the Province

Article 1.—The province of Guayaquil is free and independent; it adheres to the Catholic religion; its government is elective; its laws are the same as those of the old régime in so far as they are not opposed to the newly established form of government.

Article 2. — The province of Guayaquil is entirely free to join the great association, if it shall find it advisable, which may be formed in South America.

Article 3. — Commerce shall be free, by sea and land, with all peoples who may not be opposed to the free form of our government.

Article 4. — The government shall consist of three persons, elected by the electors of the people; it shall deal with all governmental and economic affairs of the public administration; there shall be a secretary with the right to speak and vote in case of the disability of any one of the members of the junta, or commission; and two officials of the secretaryship, all with fixed compensation.

Article 5. — Besides the common attributes of the government, it shall possess the following powers: 1. to provide all the civil and military employees; 2. to levy taxes; 3. to form treaties of amity and commerce; 4. to raise troops and to direct them when necessary; 5. to undertake public works; 6. to form regulations for domestic and foreign commerce, and for all other departments of the administration.

Article 6. — Each month there shall be published a general account of the revenues, the expenditures, and the balance in the treasury. Every three months there shall be published a general account of the public revenues and expenditures.

Article 7. — The arrangement of the troops, the order of promotions, plans of defense and everything that relates to military affairs, appertains to the commander-in-chief.

Article 8. — Whenever the country may be in danger the governor in accord with the commander-in-chief shall take measures to insure public safety.

Article 9. — After the age of sixteen no one shall be free from military service, when the safety and defense of the country requires him.

Article 10. — Only judges shall hear causes, and administer justice in civil and criminal matters. No one shall be tried by a special commission. There shall be justices of the peace, appointed by the governor, with such powers as may be given them by the latest law;

they shall have jurisdiction in probate cases.

Article 11. — There shall also be a court of second instance composed of three members.

Article 12. — The alcaldes of the towns are also judges of first instance, and appeal from them shall be to a court of second instance.

Article 13. — The disturbance of the public order is a crime against the state. Every false accuser shall suffer the penalty which the crime denounced by him merits.

Article 14. — There shall be a commission of commerce, governed as far as possible by the ordinance of Cartagena. The court of appeals shall be composed of one member of the court of second instance, drawn by lot, and of two colleagues named by the parties. The first and second members of the commission of commerce shall be elected every two years in a general convention of commerce.

Article 15. — For the internal government of towns or cities there shall be an *ayuntamiento,* a town or city council, elected by the fathers of family or heads of households. The *ayuntamiento* of the capital shall be composed of two alcaldes and ten regidores, a syndic, with the right to speak and vote, and a secretary. The alcaldes shall be changed every two years, and half of the regidores shall be changed at the expiration of the same term. The *ayuntamientos* of the towns shall be formed with reference to the population, and regulated in accordance with the latest ordinance; life-memberships are suppressed.

Article 16. — It shall be the function of the *ayuntamiento:* 1. to control the municipal police; 2. to provide for the education of the youth, and to promote agriculture and commerce; 3. to take the census and collect the statistics of the province; 4. to assist the alcaldes to abolish idleness, to prosecute vagrants

and malefactors, especially in the rural
districts; 5. to have control of the ways
and means, of which they shall give
an annual account to the government;
6. to care for the schools and hospitals,
to repair the roads and prisons, to pro-
pose and supervise public works of
utility and ornament, conforming in all
these things to the latest ordinance; 8.
to fix the salaries of newly created
offices.

Article 17. — The *ayuntamiento* of
the capital, with a proper knowledge of
the funds and expenditures, shall proceed to the regulation of the general
taxation imposed by the government,
with the right to indicate that which
will be the least burdensome for the
people. Every extraordinary tax shall
be imposed with the knowledge of the
ayuntamiento.

Article 18. — No credit shall be
admitted in account with the treasury
except by special order of the government.

Article 19. — A provincial assembly shall be convened by the government every two years in the month of October, or earlier if it should be needed. As soon as it is assembled it shall institute a public inquiry into the conduct of the government, and if its conduct should be approved, it may be re-elected.

Article 20. — The government, after the dissolution of the present electoral convention, is authorized to bring to a conclusion any items of business that may remain pending, and settle any questions that may arise concerning this ordinance, which shall be communicated to the governmental junta, already named, in order that it may resolve them or cause them to be resolved.

Dated at Guayaquil, November 11th, 1820.

———

The arrival of Bolívar's forces from the north, in 1822, produced a serious

crisis in the political affairs of Guayaquil. The Liberator demanded the in-
corporation of the province in Colombia, but this was opposed by Olmedo
and many of the inhabitants, who
wished to form an independent nation;
but as the public opinion was divided,
the government proposed to submit the
question to the electoral convention.
This project failed, however, to meet
with Bolívar's approval. No more disposed to listen to debate on this occasion
than at any other time, he issued a
proclamation, and caused the Colombian flag to be raised in the plaza of
Guayaquil. Outraged by this forcible
annexation, Olmedo, with the other
two members of the government and
two hundred prominent citizens, emi-
grated to Perú, as a protest against this
arbitrary act.

Olmedo wrote to Bolívar a serious
and dignified letter, protesting against
the action that had caused the emigra-
tion. In Perú he was received with

favour, and the province of Pasco sent
him as its representative to the constituent congress that assembled in
Lima on the 22nd of September, 1822,
and there he became a member of the
commission appointed to draft the proposed constitution. It was this congress
that invited Bolívar to command his
troops to drive the remnant of the
Spanish army out of Perú, and Olmedo
was one of the two commissioners
chosen to present the request of the congress to the Liberator. The following
are characteristic passages of Olmedo's
address:

" The Congress of Perú has wished
to confide to a delegation chosen from
its members, the honour of expressing
to Your Excellency its sentiments of
esteem and gratitude, and to express its
ardent desire to see Your Excellency by
his presence put a prompt and glorious
end to the evils of the war.

" The enemy have occupied the
capital of the republic; devastation

precedes and follows everywhere the march of the presumptuous and bloody Canterac; the trail of his forces is everywhere covered with ashes and blood.

"Enormous contributions, the pillage of rich stores and sacred temples, a blind and rigorous conscription of the Peruvian youth, have delivered opulent Lima to the fate suffered by so many peaceable and defenseless peoples, where the Tartars of the Occident have passed.

"Your Excellency has just now crushed under a firm foot the last head of the hydra of rebellion, and nothing is able to prevent Your Excellency from listening to the call from the region on which depends the liberty of a great state, the security of southern Colombia, and the crowning of the American peoples' destiny. May Your Excellency break all the bonds that hold you far from the field of battle."

The following characteristic sentences from Bolívar's reply indicate sufficiently its tone:

"For a long time my heart has drawn me towards Perú; for a long time the most brilliant soldiers of all America have been filling completely the measure of my glory by calling me to their side; but I have not been able to silence the voice of duty which has retained me on the shores of Colombia. I have solicited the authorization of the General Congress, permitting me to put my sword at the service of my brethren of the south, but this favour has not yet been accorded to me. I am in despair in my inaction, when the Colombian troops find themselves placed between dangers and glory, and I far from them. I desire ardently to proceed to Perú; my good fortune promises me that I shall see accomplished the vow of the sons of the Incas and the duty which I have marked out of not resting until the New World has thrown from its shores all of the oppressors."

After this episode, the supreme event of Olmedo's life was the composition of *La Victoria de Junin,* a canto to Bolívar. The theme of this long poem is the brilliant battle between the patriots' cavalry force of nine hundred horse and a similar royalist, or Spanish, force of thirteen hundred. The first charge by the Spaniards seemed to be successful, but the patriots rallied, and returned the charge with such fury that the royalist ranks were broken, and victory remained with the nine hundred patriots. Bolívar led the patriots in person, and this short and fierce conflict destroyed the prestige of Canterac; it was greeted by the colonists with exultant joy, and Olmedo's poem is an expression of this sentiment, a song of triumph (109).

This poem, begun shortly after the battle which it celebrates but not completed until after the battle of Ayacu-

cho, is the author's most important
contribution to the literature of the
revolution.   As a patriotic song of
triumph, it was scattered broadcast
among the people, and by many persons
it was committed to memory, and in
this fact it is seen to respond to a notable
criterion of excellence.   It is more than
a mere song of exultation; it is in some
sense prophetic, as in these lines on the
need of union:

"Será perpetua, o pueblos, esta gloria
Y vuestra libertad incontrastable
Contra el poder y liga detestable
De todos los tiranos conjurados,
Si en lazo federal de polo á polo
En la guerra y la paz vivís unidos.
Vuestra fuerza es la unión. ¡ Unión, o
         pueblos,
Para ser libres y jamás vencidos!
Esta unión, este lazo poderoso
La gran cadena de los Andes sea,
Que en fortísimo enlace se dilatan
Del uno al otro mar " (110).

The tone of triumph which pervades the poem may be illustrated by the following lines:

" Abre tus puertas, opulenta Lima,
Abate tus murallas y recibe
Al noble triunfador que rodeado
De pueblos numerosos, y aclamado
Angel de la esperanza,
Y genio de la paz y de la gloria,
En inefable majestad se avanza "
(111).

Later Olmedo was charged with a mission to England, and on the 27th of June, 1825, Bolívar wrote to him, apparently mildly distrusting the poetic imagination:

" I do not doubt that you will carry out worthily your mission in England. I am thoroughly convinced of it, since having surveyed the whole Empire of the Sun, I have not found a single diplomatist who was capable of representing Perú, and of treating more advantageously in her behalf than you. I

have, however, associated with you a
mathematician, in order that you may
not be carried away to believe that two
and two make four thousand. Our
Euclid is charged to open the eyes of
our Homer, so that he may not see with
his imagination but with his physical
organs, and that he may not be permitted to be seduced with harmonies
and measures; he ought not to be
allowed to open his ear except to listen
to the dry, rude, and naked prose of
politicians and tax-gatherers."

After his return from Europe,
Olmedo lived in retirement for a number of years, chiefly interested in his
literary work. Then the call came to
assume again public duties, but the
period of high democratic ideals had
passed; the early visions of the patriots
had faded, and the Dictators had
appeared.

NOTES

(1) Barros Arana, Diego. *Historia jeneral de Chile.* Santiago [de Chile], 1884–1902. v. 4, p. 252.

(2) Le Bon, Gustave. *Les lois psychologiques de l'évolution des peuples.* Paris, 1894.

(3) Amunátegui, M. L. *Los precursores de la independencia de Chile.* Santiago de Chile, 1909–10. v. 2, p. 8.

(4) Solórzano Pereira, Juan de. *Politica indiana.* Madrid, 1648. lib. 2, cap. I, no. 1.

(5) Amunátegui. *Los precursores.* v. 2, p. 10–15.

(6) Amunátegui. *La crónica de 1810.* Santiago [de Chile], 1876–99. v. 2, p. 49; *see also* Moses, Bernard. *Spain's declining power in South America.* University of California, 1919. p. 233–240.

(7) During the last decade of the eighteenth century practical restrictions on importing books into the Spanish colonies were to a certain extent relaxed. In 1794 there were received in Venezuela from the Peninsula seventy-seven cases of books, seventy-one of which were for Caracas, five for Guayana, and one for Maracaibo. The

same year nine cases were received from foreign countries.

(8) Quoted by Amunátegui, in *Los precursores.* v. 3, p. 264.

(9) Introduction by M. Moreno to his translation of *The rights of man* and the *Social contract.*

(10) Amunátegui. *Los precursores.* v. 3, p. 37.

(11) Barros Arana. v. 8, p. 100.

(12) *Ibid.* v. 8, p. 102.

(13) *Ibid.* v. 8, p. 46.

(14) Valdés, Ambrosio. *Carrera.* Santiago, 1888. p. 17.

(15) Barros Arana. v. 8, p. 103.

(16) Groot, J. M. *Historia eclesiástica y civil de Nueva Granada.* Bogotá, 1869–70. v. 3, p. 35.

(17) *Ibid.* v. 3, p. 50.

(18) Vergara y Vergara, J. M. *Historia de la literatura en Nueva Granada.* Bogotá, 1867. p. 391.

(19) Published by Posada and Ibáñez in *Biblioteca de historia nacional.* v. 1, p. xv-xvi.

(20) Gaspar. (In *La Revista peruana.* v. 1, p. 202.)

(21) Preface to the Bogotá edition by José María Blanco.

(22) Vergennes, C. G., *count* of. *Mémoires ou souvenirs et anecdotes.* v. 2, p. 6.

(23) Delivered January 13th, 1812.
(Monteagudo, Bernardo. *Escritos políticos.*
Buenos Aires, 1916. p. 163.)

(24) Groot. v. 3, p. 330.

(25) Gutiérrez, J. M. *Apuntes biográficos de escritores.* Buenos Aires, 1860. p. 115.

(26) Groot. v. 4, p. 406.

(27) *Ibid.* v. 4, p. 306.

(28) Paz Soldán, M. F. *Historia del Perú independiente.* Lima, 1868–74. v. 1, p. 214.

(29) Groot. v. 3, p. 141–143.

(30) *Ibid.* v. 4, p. 292.

(31) Moses, Bernard. *Spanish colonial literature in South America.* London, New York, 1922. p. 570, 571.

(32) Pelliza, M. A. *Monteagudo, su vida y sus escritos.* Buenos Aires, 1880. v. 1, p. 30.

(33) *Ibid.* v. 1, p. 33.

(34) *Gaceta de Buenos Aires.* November 29th, 1811; *also* Monteagudo. *Escritos políticos.* p. 27.

(35) *Gaceta.* February 14th, 1812; Monteagudo. p. 75.

(36) *Gaceta.* February 21st, 1812; Monteagudo. p. 79.

(37) *Gaceta.* February 28th, 1812; Monteagudo. p. 90.

(38) *Gaceta.* March 6th, 1812; Monteagudo. p. 93.

(39) *El Mártir ó Libre*. March 29th, 1812.

(40) Monteagudo. p. 117.

(41) *El Mártir ó Libre*. March 4th, 1812; Monteagudo. p. 145.

(42) Monteagudo. p. 173.

(43) *Ibid*. p. 316.

(44) *Ibid*. p. 231.

(45) *Ibid*. p. 196.

(46) *Gaceta*. March 6th, 1812; Monteagudo. p. 97.

(47) Monteagudo. p. 76.

(48) Carlos María Alvear early attained an important position in the army, rose rapidly, and at the age of twenty-five was general-in-chief of the forces of Buenos Aires. He was elected Supreme Director, January 10th, 1815. His youth scandalized the *junta patricia*, on whom the revolution depended; his predilection for the army alarmed the more thoughtful persons, and his manner of representing himself as a *Porteño* made him suspected among the people of the provinces. Like Monteagudo, he was disposed to extravagance, ostentatious living, and a conspicuous display of power. His career in Buenos Aires was strikingly like that of Carrera in Chile, but he lacked the genius, the experience, and the popular support of the Chilean. He was a friend and supporter of Carrera, but was hostile to

San Martín, and on the 8th of February, 1815, he signed a decree removing San Martín from his position as governor of Cuyo. The reign of Alvear was brief, lasting about two months, and, in spite of his decree, San Martín continued his labours at Mendoza. With the fall of Alvear his supporters lost public favour.

(49) The decree of Monteagudo's banishment was dated May 1st, 1815. Not much is known of Monteagudo's sojourn abroad, but it is known that he was in France and spent some time at Bordeaux, where, May 1st, 1817, he was awaiting news of San Martín's passage of the Andes. Having heard of the victory of Chacabuco, he applied to Rivadavia at Paris for letters of introduction and means of transportation to America.

(50) Martínez, Melchor. *Memoria histórica sobre la revolución de Chile.* Valparaiso, 1848.

(51) *La Aurora de Chile.* no. 1, p. 2.

(52) Introduction to reprint of *La Aurora de Chile.* Santiago de Chile, 1903. no. 7.

(53) *La Aurora.* no. 17.

(54) *Ibid.* no. 24.

(55) Pelliza. v. 2, p. 49–51.

(56) Irisarri's letter is printed in Pelliza. v. 2, p. 52.

(57) Pelliza. v. 2, p. 78.

(58) *Ibid.* v. 2, p. 124.

(59) *Ibid.* v. 2, p. 133.

(60) Monteagudo announced that his plan was to form an "Athenæum" in the college of San Pedro and concentrate there instruction in all the sciences and in letters. With this in view he took a part of this edifice for a public library. (*Escritos políticos.* p. 335.)

(61) It is noteworthy that in the minutes of this society, Lima is not called by its former customary title *Ciudad de los Reyes* but the *Heróica y Esforzada Ciudad de los Libres.* Monteagudo's inaugural address is printed in Odriozola's *Documentos literarios del Perú.* Lima, 1863–77. v. II, p. 451–453.

(62) Minutes of the meeting of March 1st, 1822; Odriozola. v. 2, p. 422.

(63) Odriozola. v. 11, p. 453.

(64) *Ibid.* v. 11, p. 459.

(65) *Ibid.* v. 11, p. 465.

(66) *Ibid.* v. 11, p. 432; v. 6, p. 437.

(67) Minutes of the meeting of March 8th; Odriozola. v. 11, p. 429–433.

(68) *Ibid.* v. 11, p. 440.

(69) *Ibid.* v. 11, p. 443, 469.

(70) *Ibid.* v. 11, p. 404.

(71) *El Mártir ó Libre.* April 13th, 1812.

(72) *Oración inaugural* January 13th, 1812. (Pelliza. v. 1, p. 252.)

(73) *See* Pelliza's note on William Paley.

(74) *Gaceta de Buenos Aires.* January 24th, 1812 (Pelliza. v. 1, p. 153).

(75) *Ibid.* February 21st, 1812 (Pelliza. v. 1, p. 169).

(76) *Ibid.* January 21st, 1812.

(77) *Ibid.* January 24th, 1812.

(78) "Todo derecho produce una obligación esencialmente anexo a su principio." (*Gaceta.* January 24th, 1812; Pelliza. v. 1, p. 157.)

(79) *See* Mackenna's essays on San Martín in his *Relaciones históricas.* v. 5, p. 1.

(80) Hall, Basil. *Extracts.* v. 1, p. 253–254. Spanish text of this extract is at the end of the volume.

(81) Monteagudo. p. 322–324.

(82) *Ibid.* p. 345.

(83) *Peruvian pamphlet.* London, 1823. p. 67.

(84) On the installation of the High Chamber of Justice, *see* the *Gaceta de Lima.* October 10th, 1821. Translation published in *Peruvian pamphlet.* p. 78–84, in the British museum.

(85) *Peruvian pamphlet.* p. 697.

(86) *Provisional Statute,* granted by the Protector of the Liberty of Perú, for the better administration of the free departments, and till the permanent constitution of the state is established. This was dated at Lima, October 8th, 1821, and was signed by

José de San Martín
Juan García del Río
Bernardo Monteagudo
Hipólito Unánue.

The document, in English translation, is found in *Peruvian pamphlet.* p. 68–76.

(87) As noted by Paz Soldán. v. 1, p. 303.

(88) Acosta de Samper, Soledad. *Biografía de General Antonio Nariño.* Bogotá, 1916. p. 91. Vergara y Vergara, José María. *Vida y escritos de don Antonio Nariño.* Nariño's views on centralization were embodied in a document communicated to the Supreme Junta from Cartagena. (Acosta de Samper. p. 92.) The activity at Bogotá, Popayán, Cartagena, and Antioquía increased with the growing intensity of the political propaganda. Vergara notes the fact that *Aurora* was a common designation for publications in New Granada, as it was the name of the first periodical in Chile. In *La Bagatela* Nariño opposed the ideas of federation, and urged the necessity of putting an end to the disorder that prevailed in many parts of the Republic. Nariño's project for a central government for the whole Republic presented a question concerning which the inhabitants were separated into two parties, whose hostility culminated in a combat in Bogotá on the 9th of January,

1813, in which the Federal troops were directed under Baraya.

(89) Groot. v. 3, p. 242.

(90) Bolívar, Simón. *Cartas de Bolívar, 1799 a 1822.* Paris [1895?]. p. 146, 147. This notable letter is announced as, "a un caballero que tomaba gran interés en la causa republicana de la América del Sur." In this volume it occupies p. 131–152.

(91) *Ibid.* p. 147.

(92) *Ibid.* p. 147.

(93) *Ibid.* p. 144.

(94) *Ibid.* p. 153.

(95) *Ibid.* p. 286.

(96) *Ibid.* p. 150.

(97) Pombo and Guerra. *Constituciones de Colombia.* v. 2, p. 681.

(98) *Ibid.* v. 2, p. 681–685. An English translation of Bolívar's Angostura address is found in the British museum library.

(99) Bolívar's famous letter from Kingston, Jamaica, September 6th, 1815. (*Cartas de Bolívar.* p. 144.)

(100) Letter to Pedro Gual, February 10th, 1815. (*Cartas de Bolívar.* p. 110.)

(101) It is printed in Pombo and Guerra. *Constituciones de Colombia.* v. 2, p. 716–759

(102) *See* Preliminary address to *Proyecto de constitución.* Buenos Aires, 1826.

(103) *Ibid.* p. 4.

(104) *Ibid.* p. 6.

(105) *Ibid.* p. 7.

(106) *Ibid.* p. 7–11; *Const. Art.* p. 76–90. Antonio Leocadio Guzmán's *Ojeada al proyecto de constitución que el Libertador ha presentado a la República de Bolivia.* Caracas, 1826, is a comment sometimes extravagant in its approval.

(107) Pombo and Guerra. v. 2, p. 767.

(108) *Ibid.* v. 2, p. 798–800.

(109) French translation of it is found in Rendon's *Olmedo.* Paris, 1904. p. 147–187. For the Spanish text *see* Olmedo, J. J. *Poesías.* Paris, Garnier hermanos [*pref. date* 1895].

(110) This glory, O Peoples, shall be perpetual and your liberty inextinguishable in the face of the power and the detestable league of all the sworn tyrants, if you live in war and peace united in federal bonds that reach from pole to pole.

Your force is in union, Union, O Peoples, to be free and never subdued. Let the great chain of the Andes be this union, this powerful bond, expanding in mighty links from sea to sea.

(111) Open thy gates, Oh opulent Lima; break down thy walls and receive him; the hero victorious, triumphant, ineffable, in majesty advances, surrounded by peoples in freedom, proclaiming him angel of promise, the genius of peace and of glory.

REFERENCES

Acosta de Samper, Soledad. *Biografía de General Antonio Nariño.* Bogotá, 1910.

Amunátegui, Miguel Luis. *La crónica de 1810.* Santiago [de Chile], 1876–99. 3 v.

—— *Los precursores de la independencia de Chile.* Santiago de Chile, 1870–72. 3 v.

La Aurora de Chile. Santiago de Chile, 1812–13.

—— *Reimpresión paleográfica con una introducción por J. Vicuña Cifuentes.* Santiago de Chile, 1903. 2 v.

Barros Arana, Diego. *Historia jeneral de Chili.* Santiago [de Chile], 1884–1902. 16 v.

Biblioteca de historia nacional. Bogotá, 1902–17. 20 v.
Edited by Eduardo Posada and Pedro M. Ibáñez.

Bolívar, Simón. *Cartas de Bolívar 1799 á 1822.* Paris [pref. date 1912].

Caballero, José María. *En la independencia.* (In *Biblioteca de historia nacional.* v. 1, p. [73]–274.)

Egaña, Juan de. *Memoria política sobre si conviene en Chile la libertad de cultos.* Lima, 1823.

—— Bogotá, 1828.
With preface by José María Blanco.

Gaceta de Buenos Aires. Buenos Aires, 1810–21.

—— *Reimpresión facsimilar.* Buenos Aires, 1910–15. 6 v.

Gaceta de Lima. Lima, October 10th, 1821.

GROOT, José Manuel. *Historia eclesiástica y civil de Nueva Granada.* Bogotá, 1869–70. 3 v.

—— 2. ed. Bogotá, 1889–93. 5 v.

GUTIÉRREZ, Juan María. *Apuntes biográficos de escritores, oradores y hombres de estado de la República Argentina.* Buenos Aires, 1860.

GUZMÁN, Antonio Leocadio. *Ojeada al proyecto de constitución que el Libertador ha presentado a la Republica de Bolivia.* Lima, 1826.

HALL, Basil. *Extracts from a journal written on the coasts of Chile, Peru, and Mexico, in the years 1820, 1821, 1822. 3 ed.* Edinburgh, 1824. 2 v.

LE BON, Gustave. *Les lois psychologiques de l'évolution des peuples.* Paris, 1894.

MARTÍNEZ, Melchor. *Memoria histórica sobre la revolución de Chile desde el cautiverio de Fernando VII hasta 1814.* Valparaiso, 1848.

El Mártir ó Libre. March 4th, March 29th, 1812.

Monteagudo, Bernardo. *Escritos políticos.* Buenos Aires, 1916.

Moses, Bernard. *Spain's declining power in South America, 1730–1806.* University of California, 1919.

—— *Spanish colonial literature in South America.* London, New York, The Hispanic Society of America, 1922.

Odriozola, Manuel de. *Documentos literarios del Perú.* Lima, 1863–77. 10 v.

Olmedo, José Joaquín. *Poesías.* Paris, Garnier hermanos [*pref. date* 1895].

Paz Soldán, Mariano Felipe. *Historia del Perú independiente.* Lima, 1868–74. 3 v.

Pelliza, Mariano A. *Monteagudo; su vida y sus escritos.* Buenos Aires, 1880. 2 v.

Peruvian pamphlet, being an exposition of the . . . labours of the Peruvian Government, from . . . its formation, till the 15th of July 1822 . . . translated from an official Copy printed at Lima, July 15, 1822, with notes and an appendix. London, 1823.

Pombo, —— and Guerra, —— *Constituciones de Colombia.* Bogotá, 1911.

Proyecto de constitución para la Republica de Bolívar. Buenos Aires, 1826.

Rendon, Victor M. *Olmedo, l'homme d'état et poète américain.* Paris, 1904.

Solórzano Pereira, Juan de. *Politica indiana.* Madrid, 1648.

VALDÉS, Ambrosio. *Carrera, revolucion chilena y campañas de la independencia.* 2 ed. Santiago [de Chile], 1888.

VERGARA Y VERGARA, José María. *Historia de la literatura en Nueva Granada.* Bogotá, 1867.

—— *Vida y escritos de don Antonio Nariño.*

VERGENNES, Charles Gravier, *count* of. *Mémoires ou souvenirs et anecdotes.*

VICUÑA MACKENNA, Benjamín. *Chile. Relaciones históricas.* Santiago de Chile [1877–78]. 2 v.

INDEX